A
TAO OF DIALOGUE:
A Manual of Dialogic Communication

By *Doug Ross, Ph.D.*

and Friends

A Tao of Dialogue: A Manual of
Dialogic Communication
by
Doug Ross, Ph.D. and Friends

Published by
*Createspace.com, a subsidiary of
Amazon.com*

Cover Art by:
Paul Heussenstamm
Fruit of the Soul

Library of Congress Cataloging in Publication
Ross, Douglas Alan, 1938 –
A Tao of Dialogue: A Manual of Dialogic
Communication/ by Doug Ross
Includes bibliographic references.

ISBN:1448621917

**Articles and notes about what dialogic communication is and how to do it.
Contributions by Glenna Gerard, Linda Ellinor, Anna May Simms, Michael
Baroff, Markus Hauser, Erik Oksendahl, David Bohm, Rumi, David Bohm and
Lao-Tzu.**

CONTENTS

Dedication

This book is dedicated to the memory of David Bohm, and to the Dialogue Group, Glenna Gerard and Linda Ellinor (a.k.a. Teurfs).

I want to especially thank my colleague, Jane Calbreath, my friends Howard Schechter for being such a great model and teacher and Richard Burg who invited me to my first dialogue, and the Colorado Springs Renaissance Business Associates group, who have inspired and supported me in bringing dialogue to the world.

Appreciation

Many have helped and supported me in this project. Beyond those listed above and the co-authors, I deeply appreciate the following: Barbara Lee, Valdete MacRury, Julie Indvik, Celestine McMahon, Julie Halsey, Barry Tuchfeld, Sue Marcus, Elaine Gagne, Don Dinwoodie, Jarla Ahlers, Vern Vobedja, Robin Blanc, David Banner, Margery Miller, Beth Logan, Dori and Allen Galka, Sally Von Breton, Trine Hoefling, "Dominoe Dan" Hannon, John Buck, Rob and Anita Gerard, Tony Stubbs, and my troubadour friend, Scott Kalechstein. Loyola D'Sa assisted with the second edition.

About the Cover Artist

Paul Heussenstamm's eighteen year association with gifted teacher and renowned metaphysician, Brugh Joy, led to his commitment in helping others se and experience the soul operating and influencing their lives. Paul has taught **Art as a Spiritual Path** throughout the United States and Canada for the past several years.

Fears

Fear of not being accepted.
Fear I'll put my foot in my mouth.
Fear I will come off as knowing everything.
Fear that I am too judgmental about unconscious people.

Am I talking more than you?
Is my story interesting enough?
Am I competing?
Does anybody like me?

I am in search of love:
Of relationship,
Of family,
Of myself.
Who am I?

To find out
I think I'll have to sit
And wait for time to go by
While I am being whatever
It is that I am.
And it won't be who they think I am.

No. It will be me being me.
Be me doing what I do,
Sometimes not so pretty,
Not so nice.

Not always very sensitive.
Not as compassionate
As I wish I was.
Not such a great listener.
It is knowing about many things.
And sometimes all of those!

It is being a little too blunt with feedback.
It is being angry. It is being afraid
Of myself, my power, my strength.

I am enough.
I am enough.
Be still, and wait.

-Doug Ross

Preface – Doug Ross

Before I knew what would be in it I knew I wanted to write this Tao-like book about how to dialogue. I knew it would be a labor of love, because I love dialogue - the "thought" process that David Bohm believed would make life better in our unfolding universe. I love it because it is a spiritual path for me, a great communications model for couples, a way to unearth similarities and differences among business partners, a path to wholeness, and a "profoundly different way to meet" (Peter Senge, 1992).

I had some meditations from my friend, mentor, and colleague Glenna Gerard that inspired me. I remember once when she was thinking of writing a small book and she asked some of us from what I will call the "Pajaro Group" to write to her about what dialogue meant to us on a soul and spirit level. My early attempts showed the effects of long years being scientifically analytical, but I wanted to speak from the heart, and she was inviting it. How could I refuse? Some of my hopefully more evolved writings are actually the core of this book.

At first I just wanted to get together some of my favorite pieces in one place. I wanted it to be "dialogic", and that meant to me to represent different voices. Linda Ellinor, Anna May Simms from the Pajaro Group and also from the Center for Dialogic Communication, My friend Marcus Hauser from Austria, and Michael Baroff contributed their personal pieces. Some of Glenna's and my poetry collections also seemed to fit in.

It won't surprise anybody to find something from David Bohm here. "On Dialogue", shortened for *Noetic Sciences Bulletin*, has been everybody's popular choice. Bohm was, of course, difficult to get one's arms (and mind) around. In his longer writings, I always thought I was getting an attempt by somebody who understood the universe in all its complexity making every effort to reduce it for minds not quite as ambitious as his. I don't find it so easy to reduce.

Glenna has helped me with conceptualizing how this might emerge. My goal is to explore dialogue and say what it is to me and what it is from my friends who love it as much as I do. My purpose is to allow others to see these glimpses and to allow them to weigh in about what it is for them. I imagine this as a hand-along book, and not a cash cow for me, though I hope to use it to help support my own consulting practice. It is my plan to list it among products available to those wanting some guidelines for getting dialogue groups started. Along these lines, some of the pieces were actually prepared by for a Day of Dialogue event in October 1996.

"What this book isn't" is a reader of longer published articles, of which there are several out there which could be helpful. In addition to the Bohm bibliography, *Vision/Action*, the journal of the Bay Area Organizational Development Network (BAODN), Summer, 1994, published several articles together. Sarita Chawla followed up in the Winter 1994 issue. Senge, and his colleague Bill Isaacs, have spoken and written of the value of dialogue, Joseph Jaworski, Margaret Wheatley and many others are joining their voices. I recommend them all.

So as Glenna asks in one of her meditations, "Dialogue, what are you to me?" Today my answer is that you are my spiritual path. How did you get there? I recall that when I first came to study Organizational Development and Transformation at the California Institute for

Integral Studies many classes were held in a circle and began with a check-in. Howard Schechter and Lisa Faithorn, both on the faculty, had sent me an article on using the "talking stick" in meetings. People around me were talking of the tribal council, and I noticed that all these things taken together were making me feel very much at home. I sensed that I was experiencing real community, and I liked it!

I discovered later that David Bohm had thought that dialogue wasn't anything new in the universe and is based on laws of Physics, but also a modern version of how the hunter and gatherer tribes had gotten together to plan and do business. When I found "Dialogue" on the agenda of the ODN Conference in Toronto in 1992, I couldn't stay away from it. I was tremendously curious about how Gerard and Teurfs would present and practice this quantum tribal council idea. Before I went to Toronto, thanks to friend Richard Burg, I connected with a dialogue group in Marin County and felt from the start that I understood what it was all about.

The Marin group had several members who had experienced David Bohm in presentations he made at Ojai or in conjunction with Krishnamurti at the Krishnamurti Foundation. These folks were practicing diligently and provided me with an excellent opportunity to try it myself. We met for two day weekends every other month and I learned much. It was a very intellectual experience with intense focus on thought and David's methods.

The Dialogue Group (Linda Teurfs and Glenna Gerard) seemed to me to have a broader definition of dialogue. Training included nonverbal opportunities, collage making, musical expression, physical movement, and most noticeably embraced emotions. The approach felt more comfortable to me, felt very much like the tribal councils I loved at CIIS, and definitely offered more opportunity for personal growth.

To date personal growth has eclipsed full participation in meetings and the unfolding of group mind as learning outcomes for me. I have learned to listen differently, with a much more open heart. To paraphrase Pogo, I have come face to face with my ego, and he is me. I have seen how often I have taken my truth to be *the* truth, and I have watched myself and others project, project, project.

I have applied what I have learned in my relationship, and I think I'm better for it. I listen better to my friends and to business acquaintances. I am still learning to be in inquiry, and to balance my usual tendencies at advocacy. I think I am more inclusive and less judgmental. I now see some of my assumptions before I speak from them!

In the collection is a piece on relationships that is directly informed by dialogue and Angeles Arrien's always useful Four-Fold Way. I include these here as I always do in meetings and trainings that have anything at all to do with dialogue:

- Show up; be present
- Pay attention to what has heart and meaning for you
- Say your truth without blame or judgment
- Remain open to all outcomes

In a recent session with some of my friends and co-dialoguers about how to bring dialogue to corporate clients, I had the intuition that our thinking was backward. I was suddenly asking the question of how to bring corporate clients to dialogue. We had been saying that many large businesses were fast paced, intense, and stressful. What if dialogue were offered as a refuge? Our pace is slowed, the emphasis is on "the silences between", we place inquiry above advocacy, and we don't interrupt or jump in or overlap. Reflective listening is foremost.

Dialogue trainings and workshops are often done in beautiful places, retreat centers, desert ranches, along the ocean, all intended to emphasize the easy quiet of nature and to allow the surroundings to be enriching. Dialogue is a safe place where I can both share my deepest feelings and listen compassionately to others. It is a retreat from the bombardment of news crisis, high competition, and the mad dash to get to the next goal on time.

In a recent session someone painted a picture of a huge paper mill warehouse. In the center of it all, dust proofed and sound proofed, sat a sanctuary for all employees to use. There were meditation spaces, a small reading room, and meeting space. To me, this was a natural dialogue place, and I now pay much more attention to location and surroundings.

Of my own chapters, I would choose *Refuge Dialogues for the Soul* and *Expanding the Truth Option* as favorites.

Today dialogue is my close friend inside reminding me again and again to value the quality of my life and relationships. It is in this spirit that I offer you this Tao, this way.

When the tide goes out
I know it will come back in.
On the high tide,
New life will wash up on the beach.
Once it was me.

-Doug Ross

The Center for Dialogic Communication*

I had the privilege to be one of the founders of a non-profit corporation devoted to bringing dialogue to more of the world. I believe that dialogue is the best hope for eventual world peace and environmental sustainability. Here is what co-founders Glenna Gerard, Barbara Caliguiri, Linda Ellinor*, Barry Tuchfeld, Sue Marcus, Peggy Sebera, Sheila Arthur and I crafted for our mission.

"Our purpose is to enhance mutual understanding and improve the quality of human relationships. Our belief is that by using dialogic communication principles, humans can capitalize on the richness that lives among individuals' diversity.

Inquiry is the methodology of dialogue. Through inquiry, metered by dialogic principles, transformation at all levels is possible, including the individual and the culture of social and work groups. It is conceivable that dialogic communication could be the operational medium for social transformation in our world today.

By dialogic communication we mean communication characterized by the following attributes:

- Authentic and open . . . speaking fully what is in one's mind and heart

- Willingness to temporarily suspend one's judgments and listen deeply
- Seeking to understand diverse perspectives and points of view
- Spirit of inquiry and a desire to go beyond a single person's understanding to develop shared meaning
- Awareness and incorporation of verbal and non-verbal communication
- Capacity for mindful attention to, and inquiry into, held assumptions

* The Center closed doors 1999.

---

*Linda Teurfs' name changed to Linda Ellinor during this time period, and you will see her name both ways in this book depending on the temporal context.

Part One:
What is Dialogue?

Dialogue: A Path with a Heart

"Does this path have a heart? . . . Both paths lead nowhere; but one has a heart, the other does not. One makes for a joyful journey; as long as you follow it, you are one with it."
                    -Don Juan to Carlos Castanada

At its core, dialogue is a communication process, and it is a relationship builder. It is an 'opening' process for work groups and organizations. It is a community building process, and, taken by itself, it is a spiritual path. Dialogue builds meaning co-created in a continuously evolving way. From the time of ancient tribal councils to modern techno-solons, our deepest felt and understood wisdom unfolds. Dialogue from the heart involves the loving listening that energizes creative thought and the amazing complexity of spontaneously unfolding intelligent action.

"... a path with a heart is easy; it does not make you work at liking it. . . . and the only worthwhile challenge is to traverse its full length".
                    -Don Juan

20

Open Window

The moment appears.
The invitation is extended.
The cauldron has been forged,
the protocols reviewed and amended.

The conversation begun
now blazes forth
from some smoldering ember
beneath our collective soul.

We can no longer go back.
And we turn to consider,
and we turn to convene,
and we turn to discover
just what we might mean.

-Erik Oksendahl

1. A Tao of Dialogue

by Doug Ross

For several years I have struggled with how many words it takes to describe dialogue. Some of Bohm's language, fitting for the scientific and intellectual circles he was in, is less easy to grasp in conversation. This Tao is my attempt to reduce dialogue to simple, understandable, and short sentences.

DIALOGUE is a process of co-creation. Groups of people allow their thoughts (includes feelings) to become meaningful together more than they ever could apart.

Meaning flows through words and language and is beyond words and language. Meaning unfolds organically among a group; it can be thought of and embodied in the growth of a plant in the middle of our circle.

Opinions and beliefs coming from *deep assumptions* of individuals form the raw material of group meaning.

Dialogue requires *identifying and suspending* of our *assumptions* as we speak, identifying our opinions as belonging to us, arising from our beliefs, subjective perceptions and experiences.

Suspending assumptions means holding them up for ourselves to identify, and others to see, and examining whether we need to keep them.

Suspending judgment requires us to be non-defensive in the presence of the differing values and opinions of others. Judgment and discernment are important to our survival, suspension is important to our learning.

The goal of dialogic communication is not to convince each other, or to control each other, not to manipulate, persuade, teach, or influence, but rather to expand information and meaning.

Inquiry is the asking of "open questions", e.g., "I wonder if . . .", "What . . .", "How . . .", and inviting other perceptions to come in. The *spirit of inquiry* suggests that we hold an interest in what we don't know and can learn. "I don't know" opens space to invite new knowledge in. *Inquiry* must balance advocacy.

Reflection between utterances, between speakers, and between meetings, allows time and space to take in new information and consider its meaning. Reflection periods are quiet and lead to learning.

We can *reflect* quietly in silence and we can store these reflections through journaling, drawing, imagining. In silence resides the soul. Journaling allows stepping outside the content and reflecting on it for the purpose of storage. Reflection allows us to notice the process.

Listening is quieting our own mind to be open to another. There is an active process of grasping the content of another mind and the group mind. Listening is also to ourselves, noticing our agreements and our edges.

Individuals will encounter *edges*. Edges are points of tension - ideas that make us uncomfortable suggest we are facing judgments. We can choose to sit with edges, stay safe in our own meanings, or push through to new realities, new ways of thinking and acting. It may be important to say one's truth without blame or judgment. Edges help us understand ourselves and more clearly define our boundaries. Edges help us to see what might be non-negotiable for us.

Asserting our disagreement without blame or judgment is a way to push through an edge. Allowing self to be angry without blame or attack is pushing through an edge. Releasing control is an edge.

Inclusiveness means that we allow that each person has a contribution to make. It does not mean that all can or will contribute equally. It also suggests that anyone who values these ways can contribute to them. There is a creative tension between *individual* and *group mind.* Both need to be held in awareness for the greater meaning to emerge.

In being dialogic, set and know your *intentions.*

Pay *attention* to what has meaning for you and what has meaning for others.

Asking for what I want is a gift to those being asked. Be unattached to the outcome. Remember that "no", is not a personal rejection. When patient, an alternative frequently follows "no". It can be better that what you wanted!

Dialogue brings us into *community.* Community is the *felt sense* of connection with trust that enables us to create together. It is a *community field* that allows for flow. Scott Peck says community develops in stages from (1) pseudo-community to (2) chaos, which is sometimes so uncomfortable that we recycle to pseudo-community. If we can be present in chaos and uncertainty, then we can move into (3) emptying. Letting the old die allows us to enter (4) community.

Community is not something in which one stays. We can come together when we need to do so. It is a felt sense in a person that they are safe, are important, and belong. The felt sense may be an individual experience of group-as-a-whole or experienced as meaning flowing through us.

Dialogue can be thought of as a practice field; a place of learning together and co-creating; a place of growing community, a place to practice loving each other and ourselves. Dialogic communication is the language of relationship.

Out beyond ideas of wrongdoing
and rightdoing
There is a field
I will meet you there.
When the soul lies down in that grass
The world is too full to talk about.

--Rumi

2. On Dialogue

by David Bohm

[Noetic Sciences) Editors Note: This article by David Bohm is a shorter version of his classic self-published <u>On Dialogue.</u> It is the 'bible' and has to be here. While dialogic processes seem timeless, Bohm was almost singly responsible for current attention to it. He is a hero in the best sense.]

"DIALOGUE" comes from the Greek dialogos. Logos means "the word", or in our case we would think of "the meaning of the word., and dia- means "through" (not two—a dialogue can be among any number of people; even one person can have a sense of dialogue within him or herself if the spirit of the dialogue is present).

The image this derivation suggests is of a stream of meaning flowing among us and through us and between us—a flow of meaning in the whole group, out of which will emerge some new understanding, something creative. When everybody is sensitive to all the nuances going around, and not merely to what is happening in one's own mind, there forms a meaning which is shared. And in that way we can talk together coherently and think together. It is this shared meaning that is the "glue" or "cement" that holds people and societies together.

Contrast this with the word "discussion", which has the same root as "percussion" and "concussion". Discussion really means to break things up. It emphasizes the idea of analysis, where there may be many points of view. A great deal of what we call "discussion" is not deeply serious, in the sense that there are all sorts of things held to be non-negotiable, untouchable, and things that people don't even want to talk about. Discussion is like a Ping-Pong game, with people batting the ideas back and forth in order to win the game.

In a dialogue there is no attempt to gain points, or to make your particular view prevail. It is more a common participation, in which people are not playing a game against each other but with each other. In a dialogue, everybody wins.

THE POWER OF THE GROUP

The power of the group could be compared to a laser. Ordinary light is called "incoherent", which means that it is going in all sorts of directions; the light waves are not in phase with each other so they don't build up. But a laser produces a very intense beam which is coherent. The light waves build up strength because they are all going in the same direction, and the beam can do all sorts of things that ordinary light cannot.

Now, you could say that our ordinary thought in society is incoherent—it is going in all sorts of directions, with thoughts conflicting and canceling each other out. But if people were to think together in a coherent way, as in a dialogue situation, it would have tremendous power. Then we might have such a coherent movement of communication, coherent not only at the level we recognize, but at the tacit level— at the level for which we have only a vague feeling. That would be even more important.

"Tacit" means that which is unspoken, which cannot be described—like the tacit knowledge required riding a bicycle. It is the actual/ knowledge, and it may be coherent or not. I am proposing that thought—thinking—is actually a subtle tacit process. I think we all realize that we do almost everything by this sort of tacit knowledge. Thought is emerging from the tacit ground, and any fundamental change in thought will come from the tacit ground. So if we are communicating at the tacit level then maybe thought is changing.

COMMON CONSCIOUSNESS

The tacit process is common - it is shared. The sharing is not merely the explicit communication and the body language. There is also a deeper tacit process which is common. I think the whole human race knew this for a million years: and then in five thousand years of civilization, we have lost it because our societies got too big, but now we have to get started again because it has become urgent that we communicate, to share our consciousness. We must be able to think together in order to do intelligently whatever is necessary.

The point is that this notion of dialogue and common consciousness suggests that there is some way out of our collective difficulties. If we can all suspend carrying out our impulses, suspend our assumptions and look at them, we are all in the same state of consciousness. In dialogue the whole structure of defensiveness and opinions and divisions can collapse; and suddenly the feeling can change to one of fellowship and friendship participation and sharing. We are then partaking of the common consciousness.

ASSUMPTIONS

People will however come to a group with different interests and assumptions. They are basic assumptions, not merely superficial assumptions— such as assumptions about the meaning of life; about your own self-interest your country's interest or your religious interest; about what you really think is important.

We could also call assumptions "opinions". The word "opinion" is used in several senses. When a doctor has an opinion that's the best assumption he/she can make based on the evidence. The doctor may then say, "Okay, I'm not quite sure so, let's get a second opinion". A good doctor does not react to defend the assumption. If the second opinion turns out to be different, s/he doesn't jump up and say, "How can you say such things?" That doctor's opinion would be an example of a rational sort of opinion, one not defended with a strong reaction.

Opinions tend to be experienced as "truths", assumptions that we are identified with, and which we defend. But as long as we have a defensive attitude - blocking and holding assumptions, sticking to them and saying, "I've got to be right" - then intelligence is very limited, because intelligence requires that you don't defend an assumption. The proper structure of an assumption or of an opinion is that it is open to evidence that it might not be right.

Cultural assumptions are very powerful and you are not usually aware of them, just as you are not usually aware of an accent in the way you talk. Other people can tell you that you've got one, or if you listen carefully you might find it. But the accent is part of your culture. Great deals of your assumptions are part of your culture too, and this comes out in relationships.

Krishnamurti said that "to be" is to be related. But relationship can be very painful. He said that you have to, think/feel out all your mental processes and work them through, and then that will open the way to something else. And I think that is what can happen in the dialogue group. Certain painful things

33

can happen for some people; you have to work it all out.

This is part of what I consider dialogue—for people to realize what is on each others minds without coming to any conclusions or judgments. In a dialogue we have to sort of weigh the question a little, feel it out. You become more familiar with how thought works.

It isn't necessary that everybody be convinced to have the same view. This sharing of mind of consciousness is more important than the content of the opinions. You may find that the answer is not in the opinions at all but somewhere else. Truth does not emerge from opinions; it must emerge from something else—perhaps from a more free movement of this tacit mind.

TRUTH AND MEANING

Dialogue may not be concerned directly with truth— it may arrive at truth, but it is concerned with meaning. If the meaning is incoherent you will never arrive at truth. You may think, "My meaning is coherent and somebody else's isn't," but then we'll never have meaning shared. And if some of us come to the "truth" while a lot of people are left out, it's not going to solve the problem. You will have the "truth" for yourself and for your own group whatever consolation that is. But we will continue to have conflict. Therefore it is necessary to share meaning.

Our society is incoherent and hasn't done that very well for a long time, if it ever has.

There is no "road" to truth. In dialogue we share all the roads and we finally see that none of them matters. We see the meaning of all the roads, and therefore we come to the 'no road'. Underneath all the roads are the same because of the very fact that they are "roads"—they are rigid.

THE COLLECTIVE DIMENSION

There may be no pat political "answer" to the world's problems. However the important point is not the answer—just as in a dialogue the important point is not the particular opinions—but rather the softening up the opening up, of the mind, and looking at all the opinions.

The collective dimension of the human being where we have a considerable number of people has a qualitatively new feature: It has great power—potentially or even actually. And in dialogue we discuss how to bring that to some sort of coherence and order. The question is really: Do you see the necessity of this process? That's the key question. If you see that it is absolutely necessary then you have to do something.

We should keep in mind, nonetheless, that the dialogue is not only directed at solving the ills of society, although we do have to solve those ills. But that's only the beginning. When we have a very high energy of coherence we might get beyond just being a group that could solve social problems.

Possibly it could make a new change in the individual and a change in the relation to the cosmos. Such energy has been called "communion" -. It is a kind of participation. The early Christians had a Greek word koinonia, the root of which means "to participate"—the idea of partaking of the whole and taking part in it; not merely the whole group but the whole. This is what I mean by "dialogue". I suggest that through dialogue there is the possibility for a transformation of the nature of consciousness, both individually and collectively. That's what we're exploring.

[This article was excerpted from David Bohm on Dialogue transcribed and edited by Phildea Fleming and James Brodsky in a meeting with David Bohm. To order, write: David Bohm Seminars, Box 1452, Ojai, CA 93023.]

Theoretical physicist David Bohm takes talking to its ultimate. In the true dialogue he outlines, people learn to listen to one another, to hear each other's ideas without judgment—and learn a new way of being together. Ultimately, Bohm proposes that dialogue can lead to a transformation of consciousness, both individually and collectively.

Institute of Noetic Sciences

Today, like every other day,
We wake up empty and frightened.

Don't open the study door
and begin reading.
Take down the dulcimer.
Let the beauty you love
Be what you do.

There are a thousand ways to
Kneel and kiss the Earth.

-Rumi

3. Dialogue: What is it? Why do it?

by Anna May Simms

Dialogue's simplest definition came to me when I was asked to work with a group of second graders—28 to be exact—teaching them dialogue in a form that they would understand.

I agreed to do this program one hour per week for five weeks. Then oops, what was the tool to keep the children's attention in order that they could be available to share this communication process? Finally, the night before I was to be with the group I still did not know the "how to." As I looked up from my serious pondering, hanging on my office wall was a gift a friend had made for me. It was a group of feathers tied onto a stick covered by a long furry tail with feathers and beads tied loosely to yarn hanging from the end. Ah-ha! the tool, a talking stick. The following is what I wrote after my first session with the children.

Dialogue with the Children

I asked the group to be seated in a circle on the floor large enough for each to be able to see everyone in the group.

I then unveiled the ceremonial talking stick (much oohs and aahs) and explained the agreements—not rules—that we might agree on and that the power of these agreements where woven into the stick.

Into this talking stick have been woven these agreements giving it the power to:

- Speak and be heard
- Listen and hear
- Honor silence
- Release judgment
- Speak and listen free of assumption
- Communicate freely

We then spoke of listening versus hearing and speaking with the intent to be heard.

I asked the children to share something about themselves that they would like for all of us to know. I told them we would use the talking stick so that we could practice. They were very attentive and followed the ceremony of the talking stick by listening intently and speaking with intention. We practiced. We reviewed.

40

Then I spoke to them of respect and asked what that looked like and opened the circle to speak of respect. The person with the talking stick would speak and when complete would choose one of those who requested to speak next (by raising hands) by going to the person and handing them the talking stick.

At first they spoke of who did not respect them. After a few minutes, one of the children shared that he respected his brother but his sister had died and (giggling) that maybe she decided to slip on a banana peel and die. The other children were upset that he had made light of his sister's death and judged him. I raised my hand requesting the talking stick and said, "I feel that sometimes we do not know how to express our feelings or ask questions of how someone we really care for has died. So maybe we make light of our sadness and show our love and respect for that person through questions that are silly but really mean that we want to know about what happened to this person we have lost to death."

Because of this child's sharing and the children being willing to listen in a new way, many of the children then spoke of deaths in their family; of grandparents who they had respected, of uncles, friends and pets they had lost to death. They spoke of how they remembered them with respect and how, by speaking of them, we all came to realize that this was a form of respect.

At the conclusion the teacher spent time with me and expressed how delighted she was with the children's responsiveness, how openly they had shared, and their attentiveness. (Especially it being one day before Christmas vacation.) She said, "It was as though it were a sacred circle, which was enhanced by the ceremony of the talking stick."

Outcome of Five Hours of Dialogues

Each week that followed we dialogued one of the agreements, as well as, subjects the children choose. By the last meeting there seemed to be a transformed way that the children experienced communication and they even reminded the teacher.

They each made their own talking sticks between the forth and fifth meeting and could hardly wait to take them home and teach their family members.

It's simple, it works. They continue to use the class talking stick to work out decisions, agreements and even "one-on-one" playground disputes.

Application in the World of Business

I have observed that because of first defining and then discussing the dialogue agreements, then asking the group to do a trial dialogue which is followed by a reflection period with the group, and then a period of questioning on how easy or difficult it seemed to stay with the agreements. As I participated in the reflection period with the group I became aware of where the resistance appeared in the agreements. This is what I observed (listed in order of most difficult to less difficult).

1. Felt no goal or specific outcome was confusing.
2. Had no idea of how much judgment we each had.
3. Was surprised at the amount of assumptions regarding the speaker, as well as, the speaker regarding the listeners.
4. The focus on learning versus competitive knowing.
5. How aware we had become regarding hearing versus listening.

The group then becomes more willing to be in the exploring with the group, in preference to simply personally. Thus the seed is planted and after four or five dialogues we have become an actual tree growing toward the first harvest of community.

Those involved find this affects not only the individual and the group as community but a new communication begins to occur with co-workers not involved in the dialogue, as well as, with family and friends. The seed of dialogue soon becomes a source for seeds to drop from and grow new seedlings.

Having participated in and observed this process from second grade children to corporate heads, and a multitude of in-betweens, allows me to see that from the bottom (small children) to the top (corporate heads) dialogue is moving toward itself from both ends of the spectrum.

If your plan is inflexible,
It cannot succeed.
Unable to bend,
The tree will break.
Hardness and stiffness
Lead to destruction.
Flow with the process
And live to prevail.

-Tao Te Ching, 76, Lau-Tsu

4. BUILDING BLOCKS FOR DIALOGUE

by DOUG ROSS

The building blocks of dialogue are:

- Identification and suspension of assumptions,
- Suspension of judgment,
- Listening,
- Inquiry and Reflection

Glenna Gerard and Linda Teurfs first created this list as part of the Dialogue Group's public workshops.

As a communications process for couples, partners, and groups who gather for business or pleasure, dialogue is about building relationships and community. Under the best of circumstances this shared wisdom serves the better interest of the group than does individual expertise or power driven ego forms of leadership, because it uses the collective wisdom of all the members. That is the practice of dialogic communication.

The building blocks are like the training wheels for the new bike rider, they aren't the bicycle, but they get you there. These are the stepping stones to engagement in the full abundance of the way of being known as dialogue.

Identification of Assumptions

". . . our happiness, satisfaction, and our understanding will be no deeper than our capacity to know ourselves inwardly, to encounter the outer world from the deep comfort that comes from being at home in one's own skin, from an intimate familiarity with the ways of one's own mind and body."
-Jon Kabat-Zinn

Our assumptions are our deepest held opinions, attitudes, and beliefs. We got these by growing up in a certain family, in a certain time and place, going to a certain school, knowing certain people, and reading certain books. Today we would add seeing certain movies, and being on-line in certain ways. Most of this we don't think about. It is who we are as a personality. It is what we learned and were reinforced for. Much of it is transparent to us in our ordinary states of consciousness. One could call it autopilot.

46

Much of what we say comes from these opinions, attitudes and beliefs. Sometimes, or often, we think everybody else has the same beliefs and opinions. We project this notion when we interpret other people's behaviors as seen through our own filters. So, you see, we both speak and also listen through our own unique experiences in the world. This is where assumptions come from.

Assumption identification starts with making these unconscious learnings conscious. When we speak in dialogue, we want to suspend these assumptions for others to see and for us to see. We mean literally to suspend them, to hold them up to be seen. So when we offer our wisdom in a group or in a couple, how can we let the listener know that we are coming from our own experiences in what we are saying?

What we want to preface our thoughts with is where they are coming from, so we say, "In my opinion . . .", or we say, "In my experience . . .", or we might say, "I read such and such, and what I gathered from it was . . .". We are saying what is true for us, or what our belief is. This leaves plenty of room for a different experience to add to what we seem to know. Notice how different it is to hear something that starts with, "Everybody knows that . . .", or even, "The truth is . . . ". I'm very leery of anything that is said about 'the truth'. "I statements" are a way to unearth our assumptions when we speak. We take responsibility for what we say as belonging to us when we suspend our assumptions.

Suspension of Judgment

"How can we work with the pain of judging? If we try to get rid of it by saying, 'Oh, I shouldn't be judging,' what is that? It's just another judgment. Instead, acknowledge the judgment as it arises. Allow it to come and go."

- Jack Kornfield

Gerard and Teurfs say in their public seminar workbook, "Of all the skills, suspension of judgment is the foundation for dialogue, and perhaps the most challenging." Judgments are about who is right and who is wrong. We are not saying that you shouldn't have judgment; in fact there is ample evidence that evaluation and discernment are built-in brain functions. What we are saying is that it is a good idea to bracket judgments, or hold them in abeyance while you listen to another point of view. It might be useful to think about when your judgments have proven wrong, and you had to change. How did that happen?

In dialogue we are trying to avoid a heated debate or discussion. Useful though such a contest might be, it

48

isn't dialogue. Dialogue is a much more cooperative effort. So I am asking, "Can you listen non-defensively? Can you put yourself in the other persons place, in their moccasins, so to speak? Could you suspend your own position, perhaps only temporarily, long enough to listen carefully and completely to the other point of view? Furthermore, could you state the other person's position as if it were your own?"

In a way we are also asking, do you not have within you a very fair witness that can take all the information, weigh it fairly, and see what it might mean for you? Could you be a fair diving judge rather than one who sees performance through the filters of ethnocentrism?

Listening

"Our listening comes from a place beyond words, although we use words to bring it forth. We attempt to empty ourselves from surface considerations, and listen to what is still yet largely inaudible. We are trying to bring forth the still-as-yet unknown link with our core being. Being able to listen deeply to our inner-most being increases the intimacy we have with ourselves, and which we find concurrently with others."

-Glenna Gerard and Linda Teurfs

In Dialogue there are three forms of listening. Listening is to another person, to oneself, and to the sense of the group. Listening is quiet, thoughtful, reflective and loving. When listened to with love and attention, most people relax and are most articulate. It is as if being heard supports you to speak better.

Listening can be deep. One can hear the thoughts behind the words. One can experience the innuendo, passion, and bodily sense of what another is saying. If the intention is to learn what this other mind has thought, the listening also includes integration of the new with the old. Inside you can hear yourself comparing what has been said with your own templates, testing ideas against your own experience, judging what has been said against your values, and exploring the new and creative. This is the inner journey.

I have on occasion consciously decided to listen trough a whole two hour dialogue. Difficult though it has been, it has offered profound realizations. What I am thinking is often said by another.

Another revelation is that even if what I have thought I might say isn't spoken, it may well happen that the subject recycles and there is an even better place for it. It has also happened that the dialogue has gone somewhere I could never have guessed. When listening, one can sit in wonder at the flow. And that takes us to listening to the whole, or to the group mind.

Listening to the whole, to the hologram as David Bohm sometimes called it, is a rare experience. Most of us probably don't listen to the sense of a group. Consensus builders do this well. They can move to an objective listening position and capture the sense of what several people are saying. The unfolding of meaning among a group of people is one of the central reasons for dialogic communication. Listening is at the core of this idea that meaning unfolds among us, and is shared by all of us. These moments of group coherence and creative production is usually far more inclusive than old paradigm authoritarian power packages.

In a recent training program, participants reflected that because of the silences and listening in a new way, it was possible to see possibly reactive moments, sit with it, and let it pass. It seemed profound to them.

"So it seems that silence is essential to bring about coherence and wholeness."

-David Bohm

Active listening helps another fully express himself or herself. Dialogic listening appears to be more passive. The quieter, attentive and loving listening characteristic of dialogue creates a safe zone for speaking, and allows the speaker to proceed at her/his own pace. There is plenty of time.

Dialogic listening encourages the speaker. When we are truly attended to when we are speaking to others, we seem to be able to articulate our ideas more easily. It is as if the listening empowers us to leave past blocks and anxieties behind. It also reminds me that when someone speaks often, at great length, or inappropriately, they are signaling that they have not been heard at sometime in the past. The very people who are most difficult to hear are those who need most to be listened to. Angeles Arrien teaches conflict resolution professionals to listen to such people for at least five minutes, even if you have to watch their lips move instead of listen to the message!

In summary, in a dialogue, we are listening to (1) others, (2) ourselves (both what we say and what we are thinking), and (3) to what might be called group mind. It is this group mind Bohm thought could unfold new and creative ideas.

Inquiry and Reflection

"The questioner is just as important as the one answering. A wise person is not a fount of knowledge. On the contrary, he or she is helpless until someone asks a question great enough to evoke a profound response. A person does not have wisdom. Wisdom literally happens – comes to be in the between."
-Maurice Friedman

Inquiry holds the sense of being open to new learning. Inquiry is both of ourselves, asking if we can be open to the new or different belief, opinion, or judgment, and also it means can we follow what we say with an opening question that encourages the next speaker to add to our ideas

In North American culture, and especially in the field of Psychology, there is a strong impetus to engage people in one-on-one interaction. When somebody speaks, many of us have a well-established habit of drawing the person out, encouraging them to say more, uncovering deeper or other meanings. In fact, many active listening skills emphasize this ability. While this is appropriate in one-on-one listening, dialogue asks for something else.

The inquiry process is not the process of drawing out one person, but of asking if someone in the group can add to what has been said from another perspective. I encourage speakers not to answer when they sense questions directed specifically to them, but to allow the answer to come from elsewhere. To some who are very skilled at engaging in one-on-one interaction, this process feels insulting and terrible. It isn't in dialogue, but is one of the important ways that dialogue differs from other group processes.

Along with the inquiry, reflection is often equally important. What do we mean by reflection? I mean a quiet time to think about what has just been said, to explore whether the previous inquiry brings up any new ideas, to mull over something that has just been said. It asks that all the space not be filled with words, but that there be some silence, some breaks, and some time to think. Sometimes when someone has said something dramatic to me, I may find myself gaining new meaning from it for days!

The need for reflection also points out the power of dialogues that continue over time, whether that is an extended weekend or a weekly or monthly group meeting. *The spaces between are part of the dialogue*, and thought moves in those spaces.

In dialogues, I often suggest that people journal during breaks, or immediately after a dialogue session (of about one-and-a-half to two hours). I also always build in a reflection circle at the end of each session. I think the most valuable form of reflection is to ask for what each person has learned: "What did you learn about you, about yourself, in this process today?" In more experienced groups, we might also want to reflect on group coherence, whether there were incidents of group mind emerging, whether some new thought was created. Reflection requires some silence, and it is one reason why dialogue is a quieter, slower process.

Part Two: How Do We Do It?

*"The journey of a thousand miles begins
with a single step."*

-Tao Te Ching, 64 Lao-Tzu

5. Dialogue: An Introduction

by The Dialogue Group

"Suppose we were able to share meanings freely without a compulsive urge to impose our view or to conform to those of others and without distortion and self-deception. Would this not constitute a real revolution in culture?"

- David Bohm, Changing Consciousness, 1992

Dialogue is about what we value and how we define it. It is about discovering what our true values are, about looking beyond the superficial and automatic answers to our questions. Dialogue is about expanding our capacity for attention, awareness and learning with and from each other. It is about exploring the frontiers of what it means to be human, in relationship to each other and our world.

- Glenna Gerard, 1995.

Dialogue: Something Old, Something New

David Bohm traces the roots of Dialogue to the Greek "dia" and "logos" which means "through meaning." One might think of Dialogue as a stream of meaning flowing among and through a group of people, out of which may emerge some new understanding, something creative. Dialogue moves beyond any one individual's understanding, to make explicit the implicit and build collective meaning and community.

It is useful to contrast Dialogue with discussion. In Dialogue we are interested in creating a fuller picture of reality rather than breaking it down into fragments or parts, as happens in discussion. In Dialogue we do not try to convince others of our points of view. There is no emphasis on winning, but rather on learning, collaboration and the synthesis of points of view. By employing deeper levels of listening and reflection dialogue slows down the speed at which most groups converse.

Another important aspect of Dialogue is its open-endedness. This means letting go of the need for specific results. This does not mean there are no results from Dialogue; in fact there are many. However, in releasing the need for certain predetermined outcomes, important issues can be allowed to surface which often go undiscovered in agenda based meetings. The result is often a deeper level of understanding and new insight.

A final important aspect of Dialogue is that it creates a community-based culture of cooperation and shared leadership. It moves groups from the dependency, competition and exclusion often found in hierarchical cultures to increased collaboration, partnership and inclusion.

Skill Building Blocks and Guidelines for Dialogue

The building blocks and behavioral guidelines outlined below are concepts that form scaffolding for dialogue. Like the scaffolding used in construction in the initial stages of building, they are meant to help provide an environment conducive to unfolding the dialogic process.

Rather than a set of rules, you might think of them as reminders of the level of attention which lies at the core of dialogue:

- Attention to our thinking, our feelings, our communication, assumptions and judgments;

- Attention to the unfolding meaning of the group, the spirit of inquiry and the pauses for reflection that lead to learning and understanding.

Held lightly, these guidelines and building blocks will help you enter into dialogue. Dialogue is a living process which requires the willingness of all participants to be open to letting go of the known in order to discover new perspectives and understanding. As one writer so eloquently put it, "We must be prepared in each moment to give up (our ideas of) who we are to discover all we may become."

So by all means use these guidelines to help you begin your exploration of dialogue, and in each moment, be prepared to release them and let your attention guide you to the next level of learning.

Interlocking Building Blocks: Weaving the Dialogue

[The building blocks were described in Chapter 4: *Suspension of Judgment, Assumption Identification, Listening, Inquiry and Reflection.*]

Each of the building blocks is an integral part of the dialogue. They are living parts which, like the organs of our bodies, constantly work to support the form they are part of. In each moment, the building blocks both create the context within which the dialogue unfolds and act as catalysts to support the unfolding itself. The more consciously we use them, the more they help us to enter into and sustain the dialogue.

The skills are interrelated. For example, as we begin to draw aside the curtains of our judgments, we develop the capacity to speak and listen without the automatic coloring of past thought patterns. We become less reactive, more aware of the assumptions through which we filter our observations. Choosing to suspend these assumptions, we may experiment with expanding the horizons of our perceptions, increasing the number of points of view available to us. We enter into dialogue by creating space to reflect on what we are perceiving, by seeking the next level of inquiry; and by opening up our senses and listening deeply with the intention to discover and understand.

BEHAVIORS THAT SUPPORT DIALOGUE

- ### Listening and speaking with judgment suspended
When we listen and suspend judgment we open the door to expanded understanding. When we speak without judgment we open the door for others to listen to us.

- ### Respect for differences (diversity)
Our respect is grounded in the belief that everyone has an essential contribution to make and is to be honored for the perspective that only they can bring.

- ***Role and status suspension***

Again, in dialogue, all participants and their contributions are absolutely essential to developing an integrated world view. No one perspective is more important than any other. Dialogue is about *power with*, versus power over or power under.

- ***Balancing inquiry and advocacy***

In dialogue we inquire to discover and understand others' perspectives and ideas and we advocate offering our own for consideration. The intention is to bring forth and make visible assumptions, relationships and gain new insight and understanding. It is more common for us to try to convince others of our positions. Therefore a good place to start with this guideline is to practice bringing more inquiry into the conversation.

- ***Focus on learning***.

Our intention is to learn to from each other, to expand our view and understanding, versus evaluate and determine who has the "best" view. When we are focused on learning we tend to ask more questions, try new things. We are willing to disclose our thinking so that we can see both what is working for us and what we might want to change. We want to hear from all parties so that we can gain the advantage of differing perspectives.

MAKING A DIFFERENCE

The power of dialogue is that it transforms the way those who practice it see the world; a simple statement, yet far reaching in implication. For when our view of the world changes, how we are with each other and how we create together changes as well. To borrow from Gandhi, Dialogue is about "being the change we wish to see in the world". When we practice suspending judgment and listening deeply we create an experience of respect and honor in our relationships. When we inquire into our assumptions and reflect on our own creative process we acknowledge our responsibility in creating our world and simultaneously re-acquire the power to create new possibilities.

There are many places within organizations and communities where people are "being the change they wish to see in the world". Groups of many types are exploring Dialogue as a way of building and maintaining community. Diversity work is embracing Dialogue as a way to open up and deepen conversations around race, gender, sexual preferences, and cross cultural values. It's is finding application in conflict and mediation work. Higher education is using it to explore the challenges and possibilities of shared governance on our campuses. Teams are practicing Dialogue to create more effective interpersonal communication, to inquire into difficult problems, to deepen and expand their creativity. Learning communities are integrating Dialogue into the disciplines they use to create environments that support a deeper inquiry into underlying assumptions and catalyze new insights and learning.

[The preceding text has been excerpted and abridged from the writings of Glenna Gerard and Linda Loomis Ellinor of the Dialogue Group. Please do not duplicate any portion without express permission of the Dialogue Group. Copyright 1996, The Dialogue Group. Reprinted with permission.]

6. Working Understandings for Dialogue

by Doug Ross

Many forms of group process have ground rules. Rules are too rigid for dialogue, and even 'guidelines' seem too fixed. So what follows are my 'working understandings' about being in dialogue. There are three major dialogic behaviors, speaking, listening, and staying in a reflective state of inquiry. How to do each is addressed, as are some 'housekeeping' processes to keep us humble.

Dialogue can be said to be the unfolding of a stream of meaning flowing among a group; accessing, uncovering, discovering wisdom. Here are my working understandings.

Thoughtful speaking

● *Be sensitive and caring toward each other.* We are here to dialogue in the interest of all of us. We hope to reach some shared meanings together. This is a request to be sensitive to each other, to our diversity of backgrounds, thoughts, ideas, beliefs and opinions. Anything like an attack is not condoned.

65

- *Give space for each member.* Some of us speak more readily than others. Others speak for a longer period of time. This understanding asks that we be slow enough that a more reticent speaker, a shy person, can have the opportunity to contribute. It could be worthwhile to consider an agreement to not speak for a second time until everyone has spoken at least once. This also means that you might not respond, even if somebody seems to have directed a comment or inquiry directly toward you.

- *Suspend (in the sense of holding up to be seen) our own   assumptions from which we speak.* Everything I think, or say, has roots in my experience, knowledge, understanding, beliefs and opinions. A discipline for speaking in dialogue is to be conscious of those assumptions, and preface our speaking by identifying them as our own. It is very common to project our assumptions onto others.

- *Speak from own experience, in first person singular.* To identify our assumptions, we can learn to speak from our personal experiences. "I" statements guide us to speak for ourselves. Avoid "we" statements or "you" statements; both enter into the domains of others thoughts and ideas.

- *Gauge whether to speak; neither dominate nor disappear.* Gauge how much air time you are

66

using, and monitor yourself. If you have a tendency to speak often or for extended periods, be aware of the need to be succinct. If you have a tendency to be a sponge, or feel timid about speaking in groups, try to speak up and contribute your ideas, thoughts and beliefs for the good of the group.

• *Honor the speaker; don't interrupt.* Interruptions are discourteous, though sometimes acceptable in modern day discourse. In dialogue, let the person complete all that they have to say, and leave a little space between for reflection and to give the more timid speaker the opening needed to go on to the next point.

• *Allow for silences; don't 'jump in'.* Silences have value in dialogue. They allow us to reflect on what has been said, especially when there is emotional meaning and content for the speaker. Jumping in, or overlapping the previous speaker speeds up dialogue, and often closes out opportunities to speak for those who are maintaining their own commitment to pauses and a slower pace.

Reflective Listening from the Heart

• *Be inclusive; treat each other as valued colleagues.* Take the position that everybody is equal here. Suspend role and status. Each one of us has a contribution to make, and the contributions are of equal value. Position and title are meaningless.

In a field like this, anyone can be included who is willing to endorse the understandings.

• *Walk in the other persons moccasins.* Hear what the speaker is saying from his or her perspective, rather than your own. Try to remove your own filters. Put yourself in their shoes, with their experiences and perceptions. Suspend your judgments. When you listen from the heart, you encourage the speaker and allow him/her to be more articulate.

• *Avoid "crosstalk, that is, side conversations.* Everyone in the group is part of a dialogue. If two people speak only to each other, even though the remainder of the group can learn from it, many will feel shut out and tune out. We often revert to one-on-one conversation style by asking a person a question we expect them to answer. In dialogue the practice is to form an inquiry so that anyone might generate an answer. A whispered or muttered conversation between two people when another is speaking is distracting, evidence for non-listening, and impolite.

• *Be aware of individual mind and the collective.* This seeming paradox is a challenge to both be aware of what you are thinking, feeling, and experiencing, and not getting so lost in self that

68

contact with the group is missing. If and when *shared meaning* is unfolding in the group, or when something emotional is going on, you don't want to miss it. Pay attention to both.

- *Suspend Judgments (while listening).* Be non-defensive in the face of potentially provocative opinions (equimindedness). We speak from the filters of our experience, and we hear through the same filters. These filters are our beliefs, opinions, and assumptions. They have come through our learned experiences. The request is to put those judgments aside and listen to the speaker openly.

- *Value the silences in between.* There are silences of importance between words, phrases, sentences, thoughts, speakers, sessions and meetings of the group. The silences are important. They provide opportunities to reflect on what has been said, and so is a part of listening. We listen to ourselves digesting what we have heard, and seeing how it fits with our own positions and interests. Silences also allow for our intuitions and spontaneous thoughts to arise. Valuing the silences slows the dialogue, and is one of the ways in which dialogue is profoundly different from other meeting processes. When difficulty is encountered, try using a 'talking stick'. Place the stick in the middle of the circle, and have each speaker pick it up before speaking, and replace it after being complete. In native cultures, the rule was and is that when you hold the stick you speak your truth, and no one interrupts.

The Spirit of Open Inquiry: An Attitude of Learning

- *Put aside "I know" to make space for new ways of thinking. Try "sitting with I don't know."* Bring an attitude of openness to new learning. If we think we know everything, we leave little space for new learning. Inquiry means more than asking questions. It suggests that we be inquiring of ourselves and of what is going on in the group, wondering what will unfold. An interesting exercise is to attend to not knowing, or sitting with "I don't know." Processing with one person or drawing out a speaker is common in therapy or coaching, but is not what is meant by inquiry.

- *Ask open questions, e.g., "How...?," "What ...?," and "I wonder if ...?"* These are the beginnings of open questions. Whenever possible, try to end what you've said with an open question that encourages others to add to your thoughts or ideas. A tightly wrapped argument with your conclusions doesn't encourage further unfolding of thoughts.

- *Direct inquiry to everyone.* In our ordinary day-to-day discourse, we engage in many conversations with one other person. When we ask a question, it is to that person and we wait for them to answer. Individual therapy creates the same dynamic. In dialogue, the question, when asked, should be projected to the whole group rather than to one person. Similarly, even if it appears that a question has been posed directly to you, in dialogue, another is encouraged to speak next, so you might well refrain from answering.

Administration

- *Take care of personal needs; honor the spirit of the "Law of Two Feet".* You can quietly leave the circle to use the rest room, get a drink, or otherwise take care of your own personal needs. You don't have to ask. The Law of Two Feet (from Harrison Owen's Open Space Technology) is that if you are neither learning nor contributing, you can (discretely) use your two feet to go somewhere else.

- *Honor time commitments, or renegotiate them.* If the group has understandings about beginning and ending times, honor those commitments or agree to change them.

• *Be tolerant; hold these understandings lightly.* These are working understandings or guidelines at best. Dialogue is profoundly different, and it takes awhile to get used to these ways of meeting. Be forgiving, and gentle about these understandings, hold them lightly. The best way to handle it is to allow each occasion of judgment to permit you to focus on your own issues around these agreements.

7. Dialogue Facilitation

By Doug Ross

What follows are some very brief suggestions about facilitation of a dialogue. While many recommendations are valid for any group facilitation, there are key differences, e.g., the use of frequent reflection.

- *Include a check-in process.* It builds a safe container. After you check in and introductions are complete, invite the group to agree on working understandings. After approval of everyone, ask if all members will take responsibility for the guidelines. Get agreement again. Encourage everybody to stay for the whole time; ask if anybody has to leave early and agree how to manage it.

- *Finish every dialogue experience with reflections.* A key is to make a time for it right at the beginning and keep the commitment. I like reflections on "what I have learned", especially desirable is what I have learned about myself. Other reflections might be on what worked or didn't work for you, how did you do with the process, and what was your sense of the group mind?

- Establish a place and space that is about comfort, safe and trusting. Whoever is hosting should focus on some of the following:

    - Can the participants sit in a circle, or at least see everybody else in the group?

    - Can everybody hear everybody else?

    - The center of the circle is where the creative wisdom of the group-as-a-whole will unfold, and whatever is there may serve as a metaphor for the emerging thoughts. Think about what you want there. Some ideas are a plant, sacred objects, perhaps brought by the group members, a candle, musical instruments, etc.

    - Is there exposure to natural sunlight, nature (a garden, the ocean, a stream, mountains)? Is there artwork in the room? My experience is that whatever people see will influence what they say and how they say it

74

PREWORK: QUESTIONS TO HOLD FOR THE DIALOGUE

For the pre-conference work, as well as during the workshop, journaling is common and suggested. Please find a resource that is comfortable for you to use and be sure to bring it with you.

Below are some questions to anticipate the dialogic process. If possible, journal on these questions before arriving:

- Community: What is it?

- Why do we want it?

- How do we get there?

- What are the barriers to community?

- How can dialogue be used in organizations?

- What transparent assumptions do you hold that influence everything you say and hear?

- What are your non-negotiables?

- How do you discover your own thoughts and feelings (e.g., in meetings), AND *pay attention* to what is going on outside of you in your group?

• What are the characteristics of other people in groups that irritate you most? CAVEAT: These are likely to be your edges!

About listening:

- Can you listen to somebody else without interrupting them, no matter how long they choose to speak?

- How are you at listening to your inner dialogue? Can you pay attention to both what "they" are saying and what you are thinking?

- What is it like to listen to the sense of a group? Can you step back and be the observer or fair witness?

8. Three Meditations

by Glenna Gerard

Glenna shared these meditations from her journals contemplates this "doorway to the unknown", and asks the questions students of dialogue sometimes seem obsessed with, "Are we doing it yet?"

What is dialogue to me?

A process for creating a doorway into the unknown. For discovering and releasing assumptions about who I am and how I am related to the world that I may expand my awareness of who I am and of the possibilities that exist.

To expand, rather than limit, the observer by virtue of her observation. To include rather than separate and delimit.

To include rather than separate and delimit. To allow meaning to unfold.

To remove the arbitrary boundaries we impose to create a particular version of reality, so that others may be possible.

To see my thoughts (rules) for what is and then let them go that more of the game may unfold before me.

To learn how to create without identification so that my possibilities for creation may be limitless. To remember my position within the continuum of life.

To integrate all levels of consciousness into conscious proprioception. I believe that we are proprioceptive, yet currently we are only consciously aware of a subset of our whole self.

For me dialogue is about discovery, about learning. Learning is the becoming of who I am; learning is the unfolding of my self, the universe and our relationship.

It is my identification with my assumptions, thoughts, feelings, viscera that limits my knowledge of my self. To be able to see without identification is to be able to perceive in 360 degree panorama, rather than one degree at a time. To be able to be in multiple dimensions simultaneously, to move beyond time/space, to truly be proprioceptive in creation.

Dialogue is my doorway to the unknown; it is the bridge across which I pass into expanded visions of myself and my world. It is the universal ocean of creation into which I step knowing that I will be recreated and trusting that the recreation will carry me towards integration, towards coherence. Dialogue is my "plug in" to a network of other individuals and the collective awareness that we can bring forth for each other. Dialogue, the bridge between me and other than me shows me our unity through the whole. Dialogue reminds me of who' I am. Dialogue is a medium I have created to facilitate my in "showing up, paying attention, telling the truth releasing the outcome, and seeing what unfolds".

Dialogue is a process for moving through thinking and feeling into being.

Dialogue is a form of creation. Dialogue examines and discovers, that it may "know" itself then release that "knowledge", that it may look, discover, and "know" again, moving in ever expanding spheres, a wave of awareness rippling outward through the universe. We are learning our selves.

Doorway to the Unknown

Last night in our unfiltered conversation group we passed through a doorway into a land we did not know, could not perceive with our usual senses and could not express through our usual avenues of communication.

Last night we entered the unknown, to us, land of thought forms unmaking themselves and then reforming. Forming, dissolving, reforming, and flowing into new patterns and realities.

Last night we let go and let the conversation carry us. Last night we went for a ride through landscapes we did not recognize yet knew well.

Last night our conversation became our art, the painting we created, us.

Last night we became changed. How? We watch now to discover the answers, to see the unfolding of another level of memory and creation.

In your willingness to let your conversation go, to speak into the void even when you had no idea what the relationship was, to allow that you were confused and speak anyway, to allow your expression to come forth, you clear the pathway for the unfolding of levels of meaning that you have until now been unable to perceive. Continue to allow the clearing and soon you are allowing thoughts to dissolve. When you allow the thoughts to dissolve you begin to become history-less. The past dissolves. You perceive the present now, unfiltered by the thoughts you have formed, the programs you have saved. You become innocent, available to what is, at all the levels.

Last night the thought form of the body began to dissolve during the last conversation as you began to entertain that this body as solid exists because we have an agreement that it does. The power of your joint minds entertaining the possibility of suspending that thought was sufficient to create the flickering of the boundaries at a cellular level. The possibility of your bodies being more composed of light, that your physical form could be composed of say 50% light and 50% matter as opposed to 10% light and 90% matter is now a part of your thought, of your being.

Our bodies changed their composition last night. We now have the thought to tune your vibration/composition to 50/50. We now are the meaning that will allow us to perceive other levels of meaning at 50/50 and "below". As we continue to allow the unfolding of new thoughts we create the possibility of recognizing all else that is enfolded in that thought form.

It is important for you to begin a parallel development of mind that will allow you to apprehend at these new levels of unfoldment. The brain as you know it is at the 10/90 level. Allow for the thought that there is an expanded perceiver and organizer available to you. You know they tell you that you utilize only 10% of your brain capacity. It is true.

Begin to accept the thought that you will now be bringing-on line more of your capacity. As you do this the nature of your brains will begin to change in the same way as the composition of the rest of your body. To allow this opening, this movement within your mind-tissue will be the most difficult for most of you, for it is there in your "mind" that you hold most tenaciously to your thought forms. This is the seat of control, of ordering, of making sense of your world. And, yet as you allow this organ to unfold into its expanded function you will see how it is integrated fully and is continuous with the whole of your sensory, perceptual apparatus, with the entirety of you. As this happens you will have the feeling of thinking with your whole body.

You will have to learn the patterns and flow of this new mind. Memory will appear to have dissolved. This may disconcert you. Yet all information is always continuously, in every moment, available to you. Where there is no past and no future, there is no need for memory to explain the past and predict the future, there is what is and the knowledge of this is always available to you in the moment. You have but to ask.

But, but, but... how can we build, how can we learn if we cannot remember what we have thought and done before? You do not forget...each moment of being becomes incorporated in the next moment. You will be the complete integration of each moment. This is the point where time stops, as does space. All is. Form requires the two.

In all realities where there is form shaping, dissolving and reshaping thoughts, there is a measure of time. It is different in the different "realities". So, as you would think of it, "time"" moves much faster where there is 50/50 than where there is 10/90 light and matter. Different space and time zones can exist together in the different thought dimensions. Many thoughts may occupy the same space/time grid. Their "vibrational" axis will differentiate them. They are within, interpenetrating each other. You can only perceive the wavelengths you can tune into. Just as your eye can only see what you call visible light wavelengths, yet other creatures can see other spectra.

In the next conversation step through the doorway with the intention that we come to you to give you a tour. This will be a way for you to begin to perceive what is out there. Set the intention that your "minds" will begin the expansion and tuning to be able to perceive the new lands you will be entering. Tape your sessions; ask for other ways in which you "record" what you are learning. Body workers may perceive the record in your bodies; photographers may find new apparitions on film. Communicators may find new verbal combinations, graphic forms, metaphors. Begin to expand your capacity to express what you perceive.

Are We Doing It Yet?

All the skills, all the preparation is for the emptying and the free flow of what unfolds.

Dialogue is the creation of a space that is empty, or perhaps one could say that it is filled with nothing other than listening. It awaits that which will show itself and ask for shaping.

It is the function of those within the circle to create the empty space, to then listen with all of who they are, devoid of past thought, and to then give form to the meaning which shows itself, which unfolds into the emptiness.

Does this sound unfamiliar? Every once in a while it happens to us. Those flashes of insight that come in the shower, or walking on the beach. All of these are meaning unfolding into a space of emptiness that we have created. We all have different ways of ending up in that place, which in the East is called No Mind, and in the West is........

This is one of our problems. We actually have no name for this space within our culture and yet it is essential to the unfolding of the next step, the new paradigm. We do have the experience within our memories, but we have never consciously given it a name or observed to see how it is that we can intentionally create this opening...so for us, it just happens whenever the right pieces happen to come together.

So, I beg you, let go of the question, "Are we doing it yet?"...The question itself is perhaps the last of the clutter we need to allow to leave for the emptiness to be complete, and the listening present. You will know dialogue when you clear the space and allow it to happen. And then we can tackle together the challenge of giving it a form and a description that will help others to become curious enough to embark upon the journey.

Let's make a pact to let go of the question...let's suspend that question and the assumption that "if only someone would say the right words we would get it"...for the next few days. Then when we have allowed the experience, we will come back and ask the question and see what answers spring from the group.

9. The Soul of Dialogue

by Doug Ross

"It really feels like you are all listening to me. I never felt like that before in a group." "For me there is really something new and different about the silences. I think it is that no other group I am in actually tries to be accepting of what everybody else is saying. Most of the time I feel like I am reacting."

I have had many dialogue experiences. I have been in intensive four day dialogues with the group I studied with at Jacumba Ranch (The Dialogue Group). I have been in a David Bohm inspired dialogue group that meets every two months in Marin County. I host a monthly meeting in my home and attend another. I am in an on-line dialogue. I have (with a partner) trained group process workers, business entrepreneurs, and therapists and consultants in one day workshops, and I have presented dialogue to national organizations of consultants, business owners, and members of what is known as the "adoption triad".

Beyond the clearly labeled dialogue projects, I have used dialogue in interpersonal relationships as a communication process, and in shadow consulting to business partners. I have made dialogue a way of being for myself in a wide variety of social settings. So I feel like I can reflect on the spirit of dialogue.

For me the most important new learning is about how to listen. Dialogic listening isn't active listening; it goes far beyond ways of reflecting what someone has said. For me, dialogic listening loves the uniqueness of someone's experience as honestly expressed. It is about using silences to reflect and think. It is also a process for learning, we say, bringing a spirit of inquiry.

At other times I feel deeply tested and challenged. I'm tested to hear what I don't want to. I'm challenged by long winded analysis, or discursive comments. On the other hand, I feel juiced at hearing someone get in touch with a deeply felt emotion, or open up to a new dimension of self understanding. I am tested by conversation that doesn't pause long enough to let me in without interrupting or overlapping. I am frustrated when the dialogue seems to have no heart.

As a speaker I feel like the essence of the dialogue experience is in speaking only for me and from my own experience. This is how I identify my assumptions. I am amazed at how often I use the pronoun 'we' and speak for others I think must see things just as I do.

I also notice that I now tend to turn off when someone else speaks for me using 'we'! I find I am getting better at saying what I have to say in fewer, but more meaningful phrases and sentences. The spirit of speaking is contributing without dominating or competing. Another key is to *not* speak when I think I might have something quite important to say. I am amazed that the point will be made eventually. I don't have to be the one to make it!

Synergy One of the goals of dialogue is to reach a place of group coherence, or co-creation, where there is discovery of something new or different. It was just such possibilities which energized David Bohm. This would be a human version of emergent structures and newly coherent fields. In my experiences synergy has been hauntingly infrequent and/or short lived. When it has happened it has been in groups meeting continuously and over extended time, and then it seems miraculous!

Judgment In most non-dialogue experiences in groups, I encounter extensive judgment, both in others and in myself. Opinions and beliefs are often projected as truth. In dialogue workshops of short duration, and even with extended attention to working understandings to the contrary, judgments about others, about their opinions and beliefs, and about ourselves seem excruciatingly difficult to become aware of or to suspend. And it has begun to happen in me more often. Like a muscle enhanced by lifting, I can suspend. Also like that muscle, I must continue to work it out.

Assumptions   Suspension of assumptions in dialogue means to hold our assumptions up for ourselves and others to see when we speak. This means, I have to *know* that I have an assumption, and say so to contextualize what I will say. So assumption *identification* comes before assumption suspension. Especially when the topic is emotionally charged, for me, it is a challenge to be aware of how many assumptions underlie what I am saying. In fact, my own experience is that while I work to uncover the assumptions I might not be listening to what others say. If I take the time to uncover and prepare to hold up assumptions, the dialogue may well have moved far beyond the place where my thoughts fit in. I am learning that my own inner dialogue is important to me and contributes to the group, even when I am not speaking!

The best way for me to identify my assumptions is to practice always speaking from *my* experience using "I" statements, or to start sentences saying things like, "The way I see it ... ", or "It seems to me that ..." My perception is that the transparency of assumptions from which we both speak and listen demands continuing consciousness and awareness, intention and attention.

Coherence I have experienced a very happy and satisfying feeling when someone else speaks and it feels as if they have spoken precisely for me. There have been times when I felt like my thoughts and another's must have been generated in the same space. This feels like the beginning of the synergy I spoke of above. When I am feeling like we are not cohering, when another's thoughts seem very different from my own, I notice that I am now making a choice. I can offer another point of view, and I can wait to see if the dialogue will shift courses, or somebody else will say what I was thinking. The latter often happens for me, and sometimes it happens in that moment, and at other times it happens much later in the dialogue.

Aligned action The aligned actions I have experienced hint at what could happen in a large organization or a work team were they to use dialogue continuously. I have seen the preparation of a meal seem to come together with much spontaneity and smooth coordination. I have seen a group move to the physical realm and carry out a physical task (like complex patterns of ball throwing) with amazing agility. The outcome (because it is what a business organization wants to see) holds much promise for the future.

I have three favorite metaphors for dialogic action, and none of the participants are likely to remotely consider that what they are doing is dialogic. They are the best of professional basketball teams, experienced improvisational jazz combos, and eight oared crews. In each case the players must know each other exceptionally well, and learn how to get the best out of everybody in the interest of the whole.

Soul in dialogue.   I find soul in the silences. Sometimes dark, sometimes light, the quiet between speakers, the occasions when someone has just spoken something profound, or with great display of their emotions, are the moments I most associate with the unusual experiences in dialogue. Silences have been very important for me. Meanings seem to move sliding easily into new realms. I have a deep commitment to those silent moments in dialogic communication.

There is where the soul resides. As David Whyte says in his wonderful poem titled Sweet Darkness, "The dark will be your womb tonight. The night will give you a horizon further than you can see." In dialogue I have glimpsed at that horizon. *(See page108 for the full text of Sweet Darkness.)*

Why is dialogue so important?   While there is much to think about in the question, the simple answer for me is "wholeness". An older worldview might feature fragmentation, power and control, top-down thinking, patriarchy, pyramid structures, linear thinking competition, and either-or thinking. The alternatives are wholeness, accountability without control, consensus thinking, community, circles, systems thinking, collaboration, and both-and thinking.

My life goals are to think and act in ways leading to peace and harmony in a sustainable world. Dialogue has the soul to get us there.

10. DIALOGUE: From Thought to Action

by Doug Ross

[Based on Conversations with God, Neale Donald Walsch, Putnam, 1996.]

God talked to Neale Donald Walsch about the creative process from thought to action. I've expanded on this idea from "Conversations with God" as I see it applied to dialogic thought and creation.

• Thought comes first, and is a creation.

• Thoughts, when followed by speaking, are a further creation, and have the ability to influence others.

• A thought spoken when followed by action is an even further creation, perhaps a complete creation.

• Thoughts spoken together lead to shared meanings, and provide the transition from personal mastery to creating group ideas.

• Shared meaning is necessary for flow-like action. Group learning unfolds from extended time together sharing ideas. We come to know each other better, our strengths, weaknesses, abilities, skills and characteristics.

•   Dialogue is about paying attention and being conscious of what each of us "thinks". Saying what we think so others can experience it and being heard in what we say allows partners and teams to share meanings for aligned actions. We hope individuals and teams continuously learn and can adjust to change in the interest of ongoing aligned action.

11. Twelve Steps to Relationship

by Doug Ross

'. . . we have only begun to explore the possibilities of dialogue. . going further would open up the possibility of transforming not only the relationship between people, but even more, the very nature of consciousness in which these relationships arise."
- *David Bohm, Unfolding Meaning*

1. Show up; be present and loving, both toward yourself and your partner.

2. Pay *attention* to your *intention*, and to what has deep meaning for you. Be who you are.

3. Say what you mean, and do what you say. Keep commitments and agreements, and also be flexible when that is what is needed.

4. Speak your personal truth, from your own experience, using "I statements", without blame or judgment. You are not responsible for the filters through which you are heard, but be sensitive anyway.

5. Neither dominate nor disappear. Share air time. Neither always go first, nor never go first.

6. Spare your knowledge; share your wisdom. Wisdom comes from inside where you know much. Trust yourself.

7. Honor the silences between. Soul work happens in silence. Reflect and inquire of yourself.

8. Listen without defensiveness, with love and from the heart. Walk in the other person's moccasins. Listen to yourself.

9. Attend to and reflect on what is going on in your own mind and what is going on in the shared mind between yourself and your partner.

10. Treat partners as full equals.

11.Adopt an attitude of inquiry and openness; be willing to sit in "I don't know". Ask opening questions. Listen. Reflect.

12.Be unattached to outcomes. Ask for what you want without needing to have it. Listen for "No, and . . . "thinking, i.e., interesting alternatives often follow the "No".

"The dialogue isn't over until sometime after we all leave."

- Doug Ross

12. FORMING A DIALOGUE CIRCLE

by Doug Ross

OVERVIEW: Dialogue is a profoundly different small to medium group way of meeting. Meaning is allowed to unfold continuously over time. By suspending assumptions, listening, and embodying the spirit of open inquiry, participants enter 'heart-space', and explore deep truths. Dialogue over time is continuously transformational.

BRIEF DESCRIPTION: In an open space large enough to hold a circle of from five to thirty people seated comfortably, a facilitator introduces the working understandings for being together. These focus on identifying our own assumptions and opinions so that others can understand where we are coming from. Judgments we have about the views of others are also suspended while we listen openly to views often very different from our own. We assume people will speak from the heart, an ancient and honored practice in tribal societies. We listen actively to what is being said, resisting the temptation to go inside on our own thought trip.

There are pauses between speakers, to reflect on what has been said, and honor the commitment of the speaker. We treat each other as colleagues with the common purpose of uncovering meanings we all are creating together, and we find the way of balancing own mind with group mind. We invite desires, thoughts, feelings, ideas, metaphors, poems, drawings, and symbolic movements as raw material for coherence among us.

It is difficult to adjust to the slower pace, and to sit comfortably in the silences. Each of us notices how deeply our assumptions control our ideas, beliefs and opinions. We find ourselves speaking for others. We feel we have an insight into "The Truth". But we are challenged, as each member reminds us of the working understandings we agreed to honor.

Argument isn't dialogue. When someone speaks as if to you, you are expected not to respond, but rather to deflect this inquiry to the whole group! You are curious about what another has said, and your inquiry is to the experience of the group. Interruption is challenged. Crosstalk in dyads is inappropriate because it shuts most of the group out of your conversation. Pauses get shorter until someone says that the commitment isn't being honored and it is time to slow down. And there are no decisions to be made.

Decision making isn't dialogue. If the group coheres around a thought, someone might ask whether something like a consensus exists, and even as some agree, others point out that it is just for now, and that surely meaning will continue to unfold.

Occasionally in the presence of cohering thoughts a very unique feeling enfolds the group. Somebody usually calls it community, and sometimes the group thinks, says or does amazing things. And it is for now, for the meaning continues to unfold.

METATHEORY: This is a classic example of engaged pluralism. The meaning that unfolds is definitively local (I have seen the location influence the content, and even which wall one faces in a room), and may spread through some form of morphogenesis to other thinkers in other forums. Diversity of everything is honored here as all voices are empowered and honored. The differences create shared visions of momentary realities!

FACILITATORS' LEARNING OPPORTUNITIES:
After getting agreements on the working understandings the facilitators join the participants and become indistinguishable from them. Everybody learns. It is important that participants understand that the working understandings belong to them, and that they can be held lightly.

EXPANDING RELEVANCE: Besides the profoundly different way of meeting together and the almost total redefinition of consensus, the process is an excellent tool for continuous processing groups in business and organizations, offers much potential for an ongoing conflict resolution technique, and is a community builder. It has clear affinity to a variety of family and group therapy forms, and has recently been introduced as an information gathering process for government.

IMPLEMENTATION PROFILE:
- number of participants: 5-30
- number of facilitators: 1 or 2
- time needed: 1-1/2 hours/sessions; preferably ongoing and continuous
- physical space needed; open space, chairs or cushions, NO table
- materials/equipment: minds, chartpads, plants, symbolic objects
- preparatory activities: some reading about dialogue, consciousness

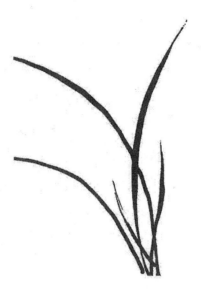

Part Three:

On The Way to Community

Thirty spokes together
make a wheel for a cart.
It is the empty space in the
center of the wheel
which enables it to be used.

Mold clay into a vessel:
it is the emptiness within
that creates the usefulness of the vessel.
Cut out doors and windows in a house:
it is the empty space inside
that creates the usefulness
of the house.

Thus, what we have may be
something substantial,
But its usefulness lies in the
unoccupied, empty space.
The substance of your body is
enlivened by maintaining
the part of you
that is unoccupied.

\-   *Tao Te Ching, Lao-Tzu #11*

13. Refuge Dialogues for the Soul

by Doug Ross

"Stressed out? No time to think and reflect? Is your work killing you? Is the stress from work flowing over into your family life? Can you figure out how to take enough time to answer these questions? Do you want to, or are the answers painfully obvious?

I propose that you come to our refuge place. We offer a group communication process known as dialogue that is slowed down, that emphasizes listening and reflection. I invite you to our co-creative world together. Are you tired of always having to compete and be an advocate in order to get ahead? Dialogue balances advocacy with the more thoughtful process of inquiry. If our chaotic work lives are fragmented; dialogic communication has the goal of wholeness and integration.

Isn't it time to do this for yourself and the people who love you? Isn't it time to step back from your work and see how to be clearer about what you are and what is important to you? "

Yes, what is above is from a marketing piece. Dialogue is a nurturing, community building way of connecting with each other. It is much slower than most ways we meet with each other, either for business or socially. I had to see it through my son's eyes to realize how little we honor our need to reflect. We are a get-busy-and-do-it society.

Brad works for IBM and he has three children. He is a two-time home owner, but doesn't live in either because it takes too much time to keep the places up. His wife works, too. She works because she is a professional and because they need the income. Neither of them spends as much time with the children as they would like, and when they do there is no time to rest, slow down, and take stock. No time to think about life, purpose, goals, values.

IBM has a conference in San Francisco every year, and he came to my workshop on learning and practicing dialogue. On the afternoon break he told me he never had done anything like this, and couldn't see how he ever could with the demand of his life systems. He works and lives with an incredibly high level of stress and is proud that he can do it.

He told me that at work he can complete 60% of what he is supposed to do, and yet he is rewarded for his work and contributions. IBM and others who have down- or right-sized, re-engineered or whatever, have discovered that if they pare the work force and keep the loyal, committed professionals willing to work long days and nights, they will be productive and keep labor costs down. But it is killing the workers and their families.

My experience and that of some friends who work with large companies and Fortune 500 corporations is that my son's experience is not uncommon. Furthermore, the same group is convinced that business is in a constant state of change and chaos. Take a look at the bookstore shelves and you will see the sages, pundits and gurus touting new paradigms, new leadership, and new values.

"Refuge dialogues" offer us a safe place to step back from all of this and reflect on it. What does it mean? Is this my purpose in life? What are my goals? How do I get time to nurture my most important relationships to spouse, children, parents? Who am I?

We slow down the pace, speaking one at a time, with silences in between to think about what was just said. We get away from competition and enter the world of cooperation and support. We allow vulnerability and fragility, and the emotions are always close by.

We suspend our judgment; try to unearth the autopilot assumptions that run us in our fast paced lives. We ask questions that encourage others to help us learn. We balance advocacy with the softer more inviting feel of inquiry. We listen and we reflect.

We listen not only to other, but also to ourselves and to what is unfolding in the group. There are silences. We reflect. Sometimes we discover some of our limitations; we enter shadowy lands where we aren't all happy, chipper and nice. It's a good sign that we are getting somewhere. Here is a poem by David Whyte from "The House of Belonging".

SWEET DARKNESS

When your eyes are tired
The world is tired also.

When your vision has gone
No part of the world can find you.

Time to go into the dark
Where the night has eyes
To recognize its own.

There you can be sure
You are not beyond love.

The dark will be your womb tonight.

The night will give you a horizon
Further than you can see.

You must learn one thing.
The world was made to be free in.

Give up all other worlds
Except the one to which you belong.

Sometimes it takes darkness
And the sweet confinement of your aloneness
To learn that

Anything or anyone
That does not bring you alive
You have made too small for you.

-*David Whyte*

[From The House of Belonging,
Copyright 1996, Many Rivers Press]

Is it time to go into the dark? Whyte says, "There you can be sure you are not beyond love." And "the night will give you a horizon further than you can see". This seeing is beyond our immediate sensory world. It let's us go deeper.

Then he says, "Sometimes it takes darkness and the sweet confinement of your aloneness to learn that anything and anyone that does not bring you alive you have made too small for you." Possibilities are vast. The well of creation awaits. Dialogues can be personal experiences as the voices inside you are finally heard, but mostly they are opportunities to slow down, learn and reflect with others who are supportive. These are refuge dialogues.

In *The Soul's Code*, James Hillman characterizes the soul as daemon, the acorn, a calling, intuition, and the eye of the heart. Neither inherited nor learned, this "how of an invisible performance" is nonetheless poised to be engaged by life. People discover this code in unique ways at pivotal times, mostly in childhood. Dialogue allows us the time to reflect on what that deep longing for ourselves might be.

My consulting practice called Collaborative Solutions and my work with the Center for Dialogic Communication focuses on dialogues outside the craziness of the business world that has my son dizzy from overwork and the family stresses caused by it. I propose refuge dialogues where we can retreat into personal and group darkness to find ourselves and our souls.

14. Opening Up

by Linda Ellinor

Imagine the following: you are part of a learning team. You are coming together to explore an interpersonal conflict that is ripping your group apart. It started brewing less than two weeks ago, and involves issues around differences in personal "style." Several members of the team are fed up with what seems to be a crisis management approach to their work. They want to engage in a more planned approach with far longer lead times. Most of the rest of the group, you included, backs the team leader's style, not as concerned about last-minute rushes. Already the matter has become highly charged. Several members refuse to speak to each other. It is time to address the matter before things get worse.

You are glad that things are finally coming to a head and that there will not be any more talking behind backs. Since the team learned dialogue six months ago, you have noticed a distinct improvement in the level of openness and trust. Dialogue also helps deal quickly with issues such as this one so that conflict doesn't fester any more. Though learning to talk openly about disagreements was scary at first, the whole team has come to view conflict differently. With dialogue things seem to work out all right once they are processed.

During the next two hours, you agree to abide by several ground rules that you have been practicing as a group. You know that when you move into the exploration of the conflict you will be free to say whatever you feel about the issue at hand.

You find yourself arguing passionately on one side of the issue. You dig in your heels; let the other side really hear what you feel. Next, perhaps only moments later, you find yourself going at it again, only this time on the opposite side. Your teammates neither find this bizarre nor you schizophrenic. In fact, several of them enter the fray with you, letting everything out on both sides of the polarity. The rest of your team members pay keen attention as the scene unfolds.

After a time, those who took sides, perhaps several, move back from the center of the circle you have formed and sit with the others on the periphery. As the center slowly empties, the team quiets itself for a few moments. Now a process of reflection takes place. What did you all hear? What is the meaning for the whole team? How can you each take the learnings that arose into your work together? Are there other aspects to the conflict that need exploration? Do they involve others outside your team, or can they be explored best by the team itself?

All of a sudden you note a shift that has taken place. Those who had refused to talk to each other because of angry feelings are laughing and talking amiably again. The tenseness is gone. Although no one decided who was right and who was wrong the conflict has become defused. It seems as if it no longer exists as an issue. Those who wanted a more planned approach to work now see the value of being open to last minute changes. Those who were more attuned to being spontaneous now understand the others' needs for some forewarning. They even see how they can provide this without it getting in the way of meeting customer needs.

After a few more minutes of open dialogue, the group decides when it will meet next and for how long. Everyone gets up and goes back to work.

Commitment to Continual Growth and Learning

What is described above is a practice available to any team willing to commit itself to continual growth and learning. It is the combination of two emerging forms of group work, dialogue and process work. During the last two years my colleague, Glenna Gerard, and I have found that by interweaving these two processes in specific ways we can speed up a group's ability to learn from the tensions and conflict that are a normal outgrowth of group life.

Dialogue

We first discovered dialogue about five years ago through the writings of the late David Bohm, a quantum physicist and philosopher. Dialogue is a communication process that focuses attention on collective thinking and learning. Practiced routinely over time it helps groups integrate certain skills and mental sets which ultimately transform their culture and ways of working together.

Through our experience with dialogue we have created ways of helping groups enter into and develop the skills essential to its practice: suspension of judgment, identification of assumptions, listening, inquiry, and reflection. What we have noticed is that, even in groups quite experienced with dialogue, highly charged conflict—usually of a repressed nature—takes time to come to the surface. We live in a society in which conflict is avoided at all costs. Our cultural norms do not allow conflict to surface directly or easily. Even in dialogue, where we can look at the differences in a way that allows learning to take place, participants hold back.

This need to repress conflict stems from a multitude of deeply seated fears and social norms. Fears in a workplace setting usually center on the possible loss of a job, hurting other people and causing interpersonal upset, losing face, being seen as a troublemaker, and so on. For these reasons, it can take considerable time to handle intense or more difficult-to-raise forms of conflict.

Process Work

Process work, coming from the work of Arnold Mindell, a Jungian analyst and physicist, is a way to handle and learn from intense forms of conflict. It employs a phenomenological approach and provides a way of depersonalizing conflict. Learning can take place quickly.

Group members pay attention to signals for what issue or conflict needs to be "processed" in their group. Conflict is viewed as a path for growth and change. The group learns quickly about itself by bringing to the surface the various polarities of a conflict. Once a conflict is identified, opposing roles are defined and team members invited to role play the various sides. Members take turns playing opposing roles and are encouraged to "try on" both sides.

Unlike dialogue, the role play has no specific guidelines or norms. Those in the roles are allowed to speak their heart and mind fully; indeed, the intent is to play a role purely—to completely identify with it and speak as though one cannot see any of the other side. The only limitations are not to say anything personally abusive and to take ownership of personal feelings.

In this way the group learns what is fully behind each perspective underlying a conflict. Conflict is defused from win-lose, black-and-white ways of working with it. The group learns together where blocks are and what might need to happen in order to move on. Each individual also learns and expands his or her ability to hold paradox by fully hearing the various perspectives expressed. This approach offers a tremendous relief valve for expressing what needs to be said. It is a safe and fast way to release emotional content while not jeopardizing personal relationships.

Synergistic Combination

After learning about Arnold Mindell's work about two years ago, we saw that dialogue and process work complimented each other in several ways and felt that their combination could be synergistic. We began slowly to weave some of Mindell's concepts and ways of working into our programs. A modification of Mindell's process, for groups that have mastered a certain level of skill with dialogue, has emerged. By working this way, groups can maximize the value of each process.

Dialogue creates a safe container in which conflict can be explored. It helps integrate the meaning of conflict as it unfolds through the group's exploration. Process work is an effective vehicle for working with the conflict inside the dialogue container. It helps to quickly expose the sides of a polarity and release the emotional content that can get in the way of people really hearing each other. Dialogue is then used to help the group sort for meaning. Through the combination of these processes group members learn skills that prevent more entrenched forms of conflict from developing. Participants learn how to inquire into differences, suspend judgment so that multiple perspectives can be formed, and uncover deep-seated belief systems that lead to conflict.

An example of how this works in real life comes from one of our recent Introduction to Dialogue programs.

Workshop on Diversity

Because our Introduction to Dialogue workshops are structured as an interweaving of didactic and experiential modules, we had already spent some 10 hours in active dialogue after the first two and one-half days of the workshop. On the third day we moved from dialogue into process work focused on a particularly charged issue in the area of diversity. It was not surprising that the issue kept coming up. This particular group comprised about 20 organizational practitioners, the majority of whom were engaged with diversity work. As with other workshop groups, we would bump up against some area of difference between us, or some issue that felt uncomfortable, and then retreat—coming to what Mindell calls an "edge."

As with any kind of diversity work, we got so embroiled in the specifics of issues that came up we were not able to see the larger outlines of the edge. Gender issues, issues of being a Hispanic and an African American, even issues of being white and part of the establishment, would come up.

As an example, Sondra, a successful diversity consultant, became easily annoyed at some of the comments of others around what "success" meant in the organizational development field. She had come from a single-parent, large Hispanic family and had worked hard to reach her position in life. There was a resentment lurking underneath some of her statements to others concerning what it took for her to get where she was.

Bruce, on the other hand, was not a diversity consultant. He was a white male in a marketing position in a small Midwest organization. Raised in the west and highly educated, everything had come easily to him. He started feeling uncomfortable with some of what Sondra was saying: "Why couldn't she just emphasize what was common between them? Why did she have to always talk about the problems she has faced in her life?"

After we went over Mindell's conflict model and laid out how we work with it in dialogue, we invited the group to address what issues seemed most energized. After a sorting process, we became very clear that the main issue we were dealing with was the one around difference itself. Some felt that it was healthier and thus better to value the common ground or similarities between people. Others felt the opposite: that until we come to value all of the differences, it is impossible to value the similarities.

Once these two polarities were identified we invited into the center of the dialogue circle anyone who wanted to role play one of the two sides. The two people who stepped forward had not yet spoken about this issue. In fact, each took sides that surprised the others in the group. Elizabeth, a white female from the Midwest, took the side that valued diversity. Jorge, a Cuban-American from Queens, took the side that valued similarity. The role play ensued; others came and went, and there was a lot of role switching. (At one point Elizabeth went over to Jorge's side and took on his role.)

After about 45 minutes there was a natural lessening of tension. Everyone could feel that both sides had been expressed fully. There was little left to explore. Those in the center came back into the dialogue circle. After a few moments of silence, we began a process of reflection.

What follows are some of the main points that came out around each side of the polarity. Some of these were made during the role play; some were distilled by the group during the reflection process. What is missing from these lists is the intense passion and emotion that these points carried and the realization that both sides have much value—and that all of us identify with each side at one time or another.

Valuing Similarity

- How can we compare what little difference we have when we were raised in the dominant society?
- There's fear around not knowing how to act . . . we can't act like all the different people we encounter. How about us? Why can't we be okay too?
- What about enjoying our similarity?
- So much time is wasted looking at difference.
- We can't "connect" around difference.
- We need a common vision. If we focus only on our difference, we will have anarchy.
- A focus on difference as identity is very difficult for people who have not come to know their own identity.
- A focus on difference can be used by those in power as a manipulative tactic to divide and conquer.

Valuing Difference

• I have to be heard and seen for who I am.
• I get lost when I have to do it your way all the time.
• Sameness is boring.
• Difference is actually what we have in common.
• There can be no trust if we focus first on similarities; we need to   acknowledge our differences.

Reflections

• It's good to hear fully from both sides.
• This gives a deeper expression of who we are.
• I now understand the other side in a way I never did before . . . Bruce's statements were so passionate.
• The whole thing was like a musical piece: differentiation at times, integration, balance point, a pulling out and then a balancing.
• A good mix of head and heart energy.

Most of us were deeply touched by the experience and found a new opening for understanding the intractable nature of issues of diversity. Most of us could see how we all struggle with our own forms of difference and how we all protect ourselves by finding comfort in our similarities, which can lead to the expulsion of others. Many of us came to the realization that we do these things unconsciously and habitually.

With the tension relieved, we found the mood of the group in the evening to be playful and almost silly. It felt as though we had been through our own crucible, had come out the other side, and now it was time to enjoy each other's company. We did.

We were an intact team and we were ready the next day to move back into the business at hand—our storming had been done successfully, and it was now time to perform.

Deep Democracy

In our in-house programs we have worked on issues that concern many companies today, including:Is there a glass ceiling? Centralization or decentralization? Standardized salaries versus flexible salaries, and balancing life and work? In every case, as there has been freedom to express the assumptions behind each polarity, the rigid ways of holding each side have softened, and the participants have increased their understanding of the issues dividing them.

Mindell's term deep democracy refers to the ultimate outcome when we do this work around group edges and conflict: full expression for each member of a group. Only when each voice can express itself does a group attain deep democracy. Until this happens varying levels of domination and control will be exercised.

Requirements for reaching the state of deep democracy include the following:

• Individuals must take responsibility for expressing their own point of view—and thus risk possible discrimination or rejection by the group.

• Individuals need to hear, not judge, divergent points of view and honor the presence of diversity within the group.

There must be enough open-ended space and time for all voices to be heard.

Deep democracy represents a shift in mind-set. Through taking part in open-ended communication processes such as dialogue and process work, group members shift their thinking away from win/lose, right/wrong ways of being with others. How people relate to each other can change profoundly and provide the foundation for a culture of collaboration and community.

The gaps are the thing. The gaps are the spirit of one's home, the attitudes and latitudes so dazzlingly spare and clean that the spirit can discover itself like a once-blind man unbound. The gaps are the clefts in the rock where you cower to see the back parts of God; they are fissures between mountains and cells the wind lances through, the icy narrowing fjords splitting the cliffs of mystery. Go up into the gaps. If you can find them; they shift and vanish too. Stalk the gap. Squeak into a gap in the soil, turn, and unlock - - more than a maple - - a universe.

-Annie Dillard

[Reprinted by permission from At Work]

15. Moving Through Dialogue

by Michael Baroff

"Are we doing it right?" "Are we 'in' or 'out' of dialogue right now?" "Where are we going?" These questions reflect the frustration, confusion and, occasionally, anger I have heard people express about what is happening or, more so, what isn't happening during a dialogue session.

In an attempt to address this issue, I turned to a model based on physical movement that helped me understand what may be occurring in the process of dialogue.

Gabrielle Roth in her book *Maps to Ecstasy - Teachings of an Urban Shaman* writes about how dance was her "way back into life ... reenter(ing) my body learning to move, from the inside out, not the outside in". For me, the process of dialogue has often been visceral -- my body reacting either with tension before words I want to share take shape, or release as I am emotionally touched by what someone else has said.

I have heard others suggest that dialogue can be an "out of body experience", a spiritual endeavor free from the physical. I, too, can relate to this experience as many times what I say seems "channeled" from some place outside of my being. However, it is the

125

metaphor of dialogue as a kinesthetic experience, listening and speaking from the inside out, and the "movement" or perceived "lack of movement" that occurs within a dialogue group that intrigues me.

Gabrielle Roth relates her experience of the "Five Sacred Rhythms" that are the essence of the fully alive body. Do these rhythms also reflect what a group in dialogue goes through?

Are the feelings of frustration and confusion we experience symptoms of our being, individually or collectively, in an unfamiliar, uncomfortable or "stuck" physical sensation, or in a transition from one rhythm into another?

The rhythms Gabrielle Roth acknowledges are: flowing, staccato, chaos, lyrical and stillness:

> *"You feel your breath rising and sinking, expanding and contracting... you ride this wave ... until you're stretching like a waking cat ... there are no sharp edges to your movements, only curves, endless circles of motion, each gesture evolving into the next .. flowing in all directions. (Then) you're caught in a sudden storm, waves pounding ... you begin to move in sharp staccato, defined ways, each movement having a beginning and end. The beat builds, the pace quickens ... you're going over the edge into chaos. You lose control ... swept up in some primal rite, falling deeper and deeper into yourself, a waking trance.*

But just when you think, you're going to burst, or collapse, you land like a feather on the light side of yourself in lyrical rhythm .. and your body sweeps into graceful loops. . . you swirl ...more and more slowly till stillness comes. "

She goes on to relate how these movements are those of the process of lovemaking and the birth of a child, and how the new physics postulates that the way to understand reality is in terms of motion.

In my experience of dancing to music that transitions through each of the rhythms, I notice at different times my body often moves to one rhythm or another more "naturally" and other rhythms require more effort to "get into".

What does this have to do with dialogue? I suggest that an underlying process of a dialogue may move a group through these basic rhythms in some form or another.

Let's begin at the final rhythm, stillness, which also recycles the complete process. A dialogue begins by breaking the stillness or silence. A flow develops as participants slowly become engaged to express a response or a new direction on whatever was initially said.

At some point a definite sounding staccato utterance is made that cuts through the flow by perhaps being in direct opposition to a previous statement or challenging an assumption. Then a dissonance of incoherence or chaos may ensue with everyone seemingly talking to themselves with no relation to anyone else. What evolves next can be a lyrical pattern in which threads of thought are tied together. And finally, resolution or closure and prolonged silence until the moment a new direction is taken and the rhythm repeats.

When "things are going well" in a dialogue it can it be said that the group is "dancing" to the same rhythm at the same time. And when "things aren't going well" can it be said that the group has lost its collective beat, or that individuals are in or onto another rhythm in dissonance to others in the group, or that individuals or the group may be uncomfortable with the rhythm it is experiencing.

Much emphasis in dialogue is placed on silence, the space between words and utterances. I am reminded of what is sometimes said when there is a dialogic impasse -- "don't just do something, stand there". This phrase itself reflects an awareness that there is a time for stillness; however, do we also appreciate that the stillness only comes after we have experienced the chaos of our incoherence and moved into forming more lyrical thought patterns.

It is my assumption that the norms of dialogue may tend to support the rhythms of "flowing", "lyrical" and "stillness" and not the abrupt changes of "staccato" (which can be perceived as attacks) or the "chaotic" (jumping in and around). Perhaps the "natural' movement through these two rhythms may upset some people's flow to the point of frustration.

To acknowledge that a dialogue group or session moves through rhythms that evolve one into another (and cycle back again) may aid in our understanding some of the frustrations inherent in the process. Acknowledging and being able to "go with the rhythms" of dialogue can possibly mitigate frustration in the process.

16. BECOMING A LEARNING COMMUNITY

by Markus Hauser

My ideas about becoming a learning community are that as a group we can learn faster and more effectively as a group, and that we could deal with complexity that is too high for individuals. As the process unfolds, several questions arise with only preliminary answers.

"What is our community learning? - To acquire knowledge? Is it learning to do things differently? Learning to be in a new way?

How can we measure learning? By the amount of change that the learning process effects, be it new behaviors or a change in consciousness?

Why should we measure learning in the first place -- to prove that some desirable process of change is going on -- to find the most effective processes for reaching a goal and to keep the learning focused ? Or is it to focus on a desirable outcome or action? It is action and consciousness changes that could eventually lead to a whole new set of behaviors.

Why become a community? So that each member cares about the common purpose and appreciates everybody's contribution. So that outcomes are aimed at serving the whole community. So that subgroups do not just work for themselves, but report back to the community. To have a support system offering motivation and resources freely.

Is becoming a community essential to becoming a learning organization? And how could a process model support the learning community? It could illustrate where we are in our process and what could likely be the next stage. It could help us explore the challenges of each stage and develop helpful tools to meet them. It might be a helpful structure for reflecting on our experiences.

What would a visual map of our endeavor look like? There must be a way to illustrate our experiences in a non-linear way, to communicate holistically.

How can we learn cooperation in learning? It is not just a question of finding a way to communicate frequently to share knowledge. I believe what is asked for is designing a process that integrates the sharing of our minds, our hearts, and our spirit.

[Extracted from computer conference dialogue by Markus Hauser (1991).]

I Am
I am my essence.
Everything and nothing, both
Star and space between.

-Doug Ross

17. Expanding the Truth Option

A Dialogic Approach to Truth

by Doug Ross

Integrity, authenticity and truthfulness seem to me to be at the deepest core of successful and heartfelt communication. Since I think communication is the crux of success in all sorts of relationships, and when it fails, at the root of most world conflicts, and since I specialize in what is known as "dialogic communication", finding ways to say my truth without blame or judgment is at the crux of everything I do.

This article is an expansion of Will Schutz 'Levels of Truth' from his book titled *The Truth Option* (1984). In his table of 6 levels he leads us to ways of truth telling in which the teller owns her own feelings behind the need to confront another. If this is successful, it is frequently only necessary to engage in the covert, but conscious process of identifying our own responsibilities in the conflict.

I will be expanding on Schutz' work, but first there are some questions to be answered. Where is truth needed? Where does it begin? How do we use truth? Is it OK to withhold truth? Is there only one truth? What about white lies? Let's proceed with some of these questions.

Where Is Truth Needed?

Truth is needed everywhere, but especially in government, business organizations, in relationships of all kinds, in conflict and dispute resolution, in a wide variety of dialogues, and in psychologically oriented "process groups".

What is raised by the question are feedback practices. In the need to confront or assert oneself, it is so easy to irritate the other party and consequently, make the situation much worse. We will see that Schutz focuses us on this practice, and it will be the centerpiece of this article.

Where Does Truth Begin?

Truth begins at home. It is commonplace to hear a person speak as if they know "THE Truth". Pronouncements declare that things are a certain way, immutably so. But this is not what we mean when we speak of the value "personal integrity". It isn't where wisdom comes from either. What is important is to get at what each of our truths is, and it may not be the same as anybody else's truth.

The way we access this truth is to speak from our own experience in the world. We use "I statements" which begin with words like, "It is my experience that . . .", or "What this brings up for me is . . . ", or

"I believe that . . ." These are the kind of sentences that access who we are, where we have been, what our experiences have been. It gets us to what matters for us, what is important, what has value.

How Do We Use truth?

The challenge is to say a truth without blaming or judging anybody. Truth can be used as a club. When we start sentences with "You . . ." or "You always, never, etc.", we are blaming and judging. This truth makes people angry or depressed. That is not why we are saying a truth. What is needed is saying what is, and possibly, how that is making us feel.

Truth is transformational, and is the foundation for relationships of all kinds. When we learn to say our truth well, and when we listen to others truths with an open heart and mind, we form relationship and community.

Is It Okay to Withhold Our Truth?

Some of us also withhold our truth. We escape the responsibility of saying what is important for us. In most cases, when we withhold our truth, we repress a strong feeling. We "stuff it". This creates resentment which builds up and then eventually explodes out of us. Unfortunately for those we love, it is frequently displaced from the original source to whoever is close by, and messes up our relation to somebody we love and who doesn't deserve this treatment.

Some say that there are truths that don't need to be spoken. Sometimes, it is best for us to let things go, not get all embroiled in the issue. Maybe it is appropriate; it's somebody else's problem, not ours.

.Are White Lies Okay?

What about "white lies". My mother advocated the use of white lies because they protect people from a nasty truth. It seems to me that white lies begin to turn gray. I do agree that we have a choice to remain silent. Maybe sometimes that is the expedient thing to do; maybe it is even sometimes noble. I fear that withholding truth comes at a cost. I always seem to have to pay.

Perception of Truth

From my years as a research psychologist, one thing I learned is that our perception of the world and events in it is never exactly like anybody else's. In fact, I continue to be surprised at how differently any two or more people will interpret an event, even when I think what has happened is clear and obvious. *So our truths are our perceptions*. They belong to us.

This raises the question for me, "If I perceive things so differently, and if this makes me different from everybody else, then is it true that only I can answer the question, "Who am I?" This we will see is a very high priority question because we are going to have to own who we are and how we have come to have this truth that is ours.

Schutz' Levels of Truth

Will Schutz teased me. I wanted more about truth. It is so important to all kinds of relationships. Here are his levels of truth, with some additions and commentary.

Level 0: Silence

Withholding information is a level of truth. While there are some personal consequences and advantages to being silent (see above), there are also strategic reasons to do so. In work settings, it may well be the only choice if you want to keep your job.

Schutz speaks of "many rationalizations for withholding: it's not tactful, it's not diplomatic, it wouldn't do any good, it will only hurt her feelings, I might get fired, he can't do anything about it anyway, I may be wrong, he'll get revenge, it's none of my business, who am I to say, she knows anyway, someone else will tell him, ad infinitum."

Level 1: "You are a . . . "

Name calling! This is a step toward revealing feelings, which are totally repressed in silence. This is full blame truth, and furthermore it labels somebody, e.g., you are stubborn, it's your fault, you are insensitive, a pain, etc. Notice how labeling makes it generalizable to all times and all places.

If we stop here our worst fears will be realized in the relationship. So the next step is to begin to say what our part in it is.

Level 2: "About you I feel . . . "

I am still thinking you are to blame, and I don't like what you've done, but I am expressing my feelings. I say, "About you I feel angry." Notice how that small shift now indicates that I have a part in this. How it is said can influence whether the other person still feels blamed, but in any case, I am now beginning to own that the feeling resides in me.

I have to say that many people I know, especially males, don't know what their feelings are, don't know the language of emotions, and don't have a feelings vocabulary. When doing trainings about appropriate feedback, I hand out a list of feeling words.

Level 3: "About you I feel dislike, because . . . "

This builds on level 2 and is a big and necessary step. Now, in addition to identifying feelings, I am going to try to explain why I feel this way. The skill here is to describe the cause. Just the facts, ma'am. "About you I feel dislike because telling me what I should do is so much like my mother, and I hated that I never got to say what I wanted to do."

It is the connection between the event and the feeling that is important to elucidate. Also, we own even more of our responsibility here. "I dislike you because when you told me I am always late, it reminded me of my annoying first wife complaining about me." When I realize how I got to feel as I did, I now have a way to resolve our difficulties.

Level 4: "I feel . . . , because . . . , which means . . . "

What is happening at this level is we begin to understand ourselves. What is likely is that we will become aware of our projections. We will see that our dislike at being labeled a late-comer has something to do with our own inside judgments about lateness, or our fear that we are actually insensitive to others we keep waiting. It reminds us of unresolved interpersonal issues we have from our past.

139

I am having feelings; they are influencing how I perceive what you are doing or saying. I have this perception because of my past experiences. I can work on those things, the reasons, and what meanings they have for me. I can decide whether I am ready to give up these old stories. In fact, if I am all healed, virtually nothing you can do will upset me! I know my defenses.

Level 5: "I fear . . . "

I fear I am not good enough, I am lazy, I don't communicate well, I have a hot temper, etc. The reason is now tucked away clearly inside me. You feel about me the same way I feel about myself. You have discovered my mask and unmasked me. I fear you will now dislike the real me. The masked man was an impostor, and only I know how much I am one.

Notice how little this has to do with "you". I am now at the place of not mentioning my difference with you. The work I have to do is with me. It could be said I am finally fully aware of myself.

Level 6: "What is true about me is . . . "

In this level (Julie Indvik's modification), I am now looking at my patterns. This new level implies that I am a creature of habit, and that I have incorporated some of these into my personality. Be careful! This need not look like self blame or judgment. It is an opportunity to learn more.

Level 7: "What would work better for me is ... "

At level 7 (my addition) if your partner is still listening, it might be important to say how what happened could have been easier for you. "When you told me I still don't clean the sink to your standards, it would have helped if you would also have recognized that I am working to improve."

Some feedback is wanted and needed, and how it is presented can mean everything about how easy it is to hear. If the person giving the criticism is somewhat vulnerable, then it is easier to hear. "I know I am really a stickler for sink cleanliness, this has always been true of me, and I still want you to know that after you clean up there are still food particles on the sides of the sink. Do you think you can include that in your improvement plan?"

In summary, there is a sequence of steps that make the truth easier to hear. Here is a final example. When you leave the music on after you leave, I feel depressed because you seem insensitive to my requests to turn off appliances and to have my own silence. This means that I probably am overconcerned about the costs, an old issue for me that comes from my upbringing. Also I may fear that I have been intrusive by making noise. I fear that I have been noisy and wasteful too. What is true about me is that I am trying to be more attentive to costs of living and to intrusion, and these are issues I am working to correct.

Purpose in Writing about Truth

I have been commended for my honesty. I have seen how truth can be transforming in conflict resolution, dialogue, T-groups, love relationships, friendships, and organizations. I see how integrity leads to trust. I have seen how truth doesn't end relationships.

I have seen that lasting friendships worth keeping were based on open and honest sharing. I have seen how trust emerging from truth experiences supports love. I have learned to describe challenging situations and say how it makes me feel. Then I have learned to say this truth in a vulnerable way so it let's the listener understand. I have been surprised to find that people then like to be with me.

I have seen that I can find out things about myself I didn't know. This is discovery of the classic "blind quadrant" of the Johari Window (Luft, 1984). This happens because when I am truthful to others in a careful way, they reciprocate and offer me feedback I want and need. Blame and judgment shuts me down and I don't listen or learn. When I don't feel blamed, I can actually seek more feedback and learn about myself.

Quadrant three is what is known to me but not to others. My vulnerable sharing seems to have made more of me accessible to others, and then *they* reciprocate! I find out more about them. Then I practice listening from my heart, staying as open as I can to 'the other'.

Honoring truth has allowed me to feel what it means to be in integrity. Being integrous makes me feel grounded, settled, enables me to be myself and to love and honor who I am. It has also helped me to have a sense of my essence, and that has given me a glimpse of God.

"THE Truth"

It is important to understand that there is no "The Truth". We all perceive through filters. We each learned different values, and our perceptions of the world, what is good and what is bad, what is right and what is wrong. Cultures and sub-cultures differ, they value different ways of being; they have different taboos.

What each of us does have is *our* truth, opinions, beliefs, attitudes, and all that we have learned. Much of what we learn about our culture or our family is not really consciously available to us. Tacitly, we learn this before we have any choice. For most of us it is a major challenge to become aware of these assumptions that guide what we hear, think, and say.

Speaking using "I statements" helps us to identify these deep seated assumptions, and helps us to know our own truths.

Given how unique this sets us up to be, the question arises, "How do we fit into . . . family, social group, work group, relationship?"

Family.   Marriages are the merger of two often very different cultures. Blended families where two adults come together with children multiply the extent of the culture merger. Businesses that merge bring two different ways of doing things together. How can these differences be melded together? Truth has the best prospect.

Perennial wisdom suggests it takes at least one pass through the four seasons to get a full sense of anything new - a relationship, a job - all the blending involved. So the first step is to notice differences and describe the different perspectives. The next step is to say how the other perspective feels, and to welcome the return of feelings.

A friend shared an interesting metaphor. The two families just seemed unable to blend in any form. He said it was as if there were two rooms in the house and neither group was comfortable in the others room. As a mutual friend, he could go back and forth in comfort, but nobody else was willing to do so. They chose to stay in their own room.

Work groups. So often it seems necessary to cover yourself. To me this suggests that you have to withhold or alter your truth. I have spoken with relatives and friends about job interviews. They often say that they like the job, but not the interviewer. It seems to me that the interviewer is formed by the corporate culture, and the work is more likely to be like the person than like the written job description. If you don't fit with the interviewer, you probably won't fit with the job. Why work where you don't belong? Find a culture that matches who you are. This will be a place where you don't have to withhold yourself, walk on eggs, or cover your derriere.

Social Groups. I think Groucho Marx was the first to say it, "I'd never belong to a group that would have me as a member." There are groups everywhere looking for members. Which ones do you fit? If you know who you are, you will know where you fit. Groucho knew himself well! He didn't fit anywhere. If conversation is halting and awkward, if you are taking pledges to do things you otherwise never would, if you feel like a fifth wheel, if they don't show any interest in you or your ideas, there is probably a misfitting. There is no need to be angry at this unless it's based on prejudice. There are some places you just don't need to be.

Love relationships. For about six months you won't really know if you fit or not. In fact, you will think you fit perfectly. Falling in love releases hormones

145

that make you think everything about this person is perfect and/or that they are just like you or fit perfectly. This hormonal truth is not the most reliable. Six moths later, when the hormones stabilize, in everyday life and decision making, questions will arise about how well you fit. Those endearing differences which felt so good under the influence of hormones now recall old wars with your parents or ex-friends. How are we going to deal with this (Ross, *Make It Last*, 2009)?

First describe the difference you are noticing in objective terms. You can say things like, "I notice you leave your coffee grounds in the sink for two or more days." You can start with this and see what happens. Usually, your partner, now no longer thinking this is a cute difference to be spoken of lightly in social situations, will become defensive. The response is likely to be something like, "You don't put your clothes away for a week! Who are you to criticize me?" Get the feeling?

What is needed here is for the person who notices coffee grounds to know how to follow the observation with a feeling statement that makes him or her just as vulnerable as the errant mess-maker. Try this. "I notice you leave your coffee grounds in the sink when you make coffee. I know you don't have any intention of irritating me, and I want you to know that it feels disrespectful of my need for cleanliness. This means I have to either clean it up myself, or bug you about it. I don't want to do that because I neither like to clean up after you nor do I want to bug you about it. Now it's true that I am very into cleanliness, especially around the kitchen, and this goes way back into my upbringing. What I would like is your agreement to clean up right away. Do you think you could agree to this?"

Do you see that what the speaker is taking responsibility for his or her own sensitivity? This vulnerable approach welcomes the other person to take responsibility too. Here would be my response to the above.

"Wow, I never realized that before. I now recall you mentioned this before, but I didn't understand how important it is to you. I don't want to do anything that irritates you because I love you and don't want you to be irritated with me. I will put the grounds right in the garbage from now on. Thanks for telling me how this makes you feel."

I have found that when in a relationship, the crucial agreement is to be willing to learn as we grow together. This isn't the last place that there will be differences.

So time and again we are asked to know who we are, that is, our truth. Self awareness has been tackled by many. Schutz offers his Firo-B to assess control, inclusion and openness. The Myers-Briggs gets at types like introversion/extroversion, feeling or thinking as a thought style, judging or perceiving.

Enneagrams, astrology, personality tests, therapy, support groups and meditation all help us to find out who we are. Journaling and then rereading what we have written over a period of time is helpful so that we don't just think that how we are today is how we always are. Nor are we the same in all situations.

I have had to do almost all of the above and then sit quietly with myself. I have committed to my truth, and I have learned that there is not much difference between truth and intuition. I have found that in the quiet of meditation wisdom, my truth comes to me.

A final note on finding out who you are: Write down the kinds of questions to yourself that consultants and planners raise for businesses all the time. What is your mission? What are your values, and how do they support or diminish your mission? What are your goals and objectives? What is your vision for the future?

Answer these questions, and then check the answers out with somebody who knows you well. Find out if what they see about you correlates with what you think about you. I there anything they see about you that you have left out. This will give you a good idea of who you are.

How can we learn that we can trust ourselves to be sufficient to handle each moment, to be enough? We will have to see that we need to put ourselves at some risk to achieve this goal. If we stay in the truth of who we are it will be easier. High risk often follows from wanting to be something else, usually, something we are not. We have to learn to stop judging ourselves. It was our parents or school teachers who made everything we did right or wrong, or good or bad. But before that we just were who we were. Whatever we do offers us some feedback about others and ourselves. That is just how things are.

How Can I Be Open? Three Laws

If we are closed to learning about ourselves or others, we will be stuck with what we think we know, our personal version of the truth. This whole article assumes we want to learn, so we have to be open. I have three brief laws of openness.

The first is: *You don't know it all.* Nobody does. To be open you start with knowing that there is much you don't know, or that others know things you don't, or see it differently.

The second law is: *Listen.* This means consciously pay attention to others and what they say. Try to get inside their heads to understand where they are coming from. Many people don't feel heard. Really listen to them. Get in their moccasins. It is also important to listen to yourself! What is the conversation going on inside your head? What has meaning for you? Why does it have meaning? Are you learning?

The third law is *don't give advice unless it is sought*. Advice makes you a "knower". After you have listened well and understand, then you might do well to identify what advice you would give to yourself. And if you are asked, you can answer, "Well I've been thinking what advice I'd give myself, and it seems I would want to . . . ". Instead of giving advice, you will be dialoguing with your friend about the situation, learning yourself, and sharing that wisdom. Maybe this will help the other person.

How Can I Love Somebody Very Different From Myself?

First know that you have a choice to have nothing whatsoever to do with some people. Most of us make as friends, have as co-workers, or have love relationships with people who are very different from us. At first, we find the differences interesting or cute, or leading us to growth, or adding to what we seem to be. Hormones make us like the differences . . . for six months (or so).

Then the differences seem to turn into challenges. What *was* cute is now irritating, uncomfortable, and not the way I do things! There is a point at which I am going to decide whether to stick this out or walk away. Now what? The other person can't or won't change, so what can I do.

Truth can transform, so I start speaking my truth using the skills we have been talking about: Say what you see or have heard, followed by how it makes you feel. Say "because . . . and "which means . . . "what is true about me is. Then listen to what is said back to you. Listen carefully, stay open, and don't give any advice. Try to understand the other person before you seek to be understood *(Covey, Seven Habits of Highly Effective People,* 1990). Say what you would like to have for yourself, and then don't be attached to the outcome.

Ask For What You Want.

I have found out something very interesting from asking for what I want. I have learned from using these principles that "No" is a very interesting sentence that all of us need to learn. Sometimes it is a complete sentence. It just stops things right there. Many people want things from us that it's not healthy for us to give. Some of these people don't seem to be able to hear dissuasion unless it is a short and clearly punctuated sentence. Here it is again in case you want to learn it. "No!"

Here is the interesting part. If your request isn't totally irrational, it frequently happens that "No" is followed by something. By staying present, and not asking for ridiculously outrageous demands, you allow your partner to suggest an alternative! Yes, an alternative to what you asked for. I have discovered that sometimes are better than what I thought I wanted! Please try this. It's amazing!

I was in a therapy session and my therapist suggested that I practice asking for what I want. So at the end of the hour I said to her, "I want to switch chairs with you next time we meet. This one is so uncomfortable!" She said, "No. I'm sorry; I need this chair for my sore back." As I started to pout, she said, "I agree with you. And it does look pretty bleak, and I think I have another chair in storage. I'll get that one out for our next session."

Not only did she validate my position, but offered a better alternative. My next session and all after that were held in a whole new facility with far better furniture! I've been practicing this skill ever since!

How Can I Impart Difficult Truths to My Ranking Superiors?

There are two issues surrounding rank and status. One is how to suspend it; the other is how to own it. There is rank everywhere, not just in the workplace and what I want to do here is simplify the issues as much as possible.

[There is so much to say here, and I won't repeat the excellent material easily available about diversity. I particularly recommend Arnold Mindell's Sitting in the Fire,1995.]

To suspend rank, ask for equality. Dialogic communication values all contributions and assumes each person has much to offer every other person. In the world of experience and individual perceptions, none are better than others. Every truth is valuable and worth listening to. Rank shuts the lesser ranking person down. This is not a good thing.

The rank we want to own is our equality with other human beings. So sometimes we encounter people who haven't read about or heard about truth, equality, or dialogue. The challenge then is how to claim equal rank when it is lacking. My suggestion is always name it. This brings us back again to the theme of truth telling. We again need to say our truth. The formula is the same.

First, describe what you notice. Second, say how it makes you feel. ("Marginalized" is the vogue word in 1998 as I write this.) Third, say why and what it means to you. Say why you don't like being made less than, and ask to be treated as an equal. Say what the truth about you is, and say you value equality, democracy, sharing equally, and being treated equally. Then listen. Decide if this is a place you want to be and make your choice.

The Practice of Truth

There follows a short practical primer of how to be truthful. Start with this saying I borrowed from Angeles Arrien, live by it one day at a time. "Say what you mean; do what you say"! A corollary is, "Think first"!

1. *Describe what you sense, i.e., see, hear, smell, taste, and touch.* Say "When . . . (and describe the event as you experienced it); "I notice . . . ." Don't interpret it. Don't make assumptions or inferences.

2. *Practice describing behavior without interpreting it, and stop there!* Here are some samples:

"I'm talking and you are looking around at your papers."
"I notice that your voice is getting loud and your face is turning red."
"It looks to me like you are experiencing some kind of emotion."

Then **stop**! Don't say anything else. Listen for what comes next. Let the other person speak. Don't rescue the other person. To rescue others is to rescue you.

3. *Describe and then feel.* After describing, either before or after listening, say what you are feeling. Say this in a vulnerable way that lets down barriers to continuing the dialogue.

"It feels like (you) . . ." or "It feels that . . ." are not feelings! They are thoughts, stories about the there and then, or they imply that blame is coming next. These beginnings lead to judgments. Get these out of your vocabulary.

If somebody you are helping doesn't seem to be able to form a sentence about their feelings and says "It feels like you . . ." Follow that by immediately with, "And when it feels like that, how do you feel? You can prompt the other person by asking, "Does it make you feel angry, fearful, sad, joyful, etc." Some of us have a limited feeling vocabulary. People just didn't talk like that in our family.

4. *Take responsibility.* This is a very important step. Understand that your emotions are all yours; they happen inside of you. Nobody can make you anything. External events trigger old memories, reminding us of past emotional moments in our lives. Then we experience what we felt before.

What people are doing or saying isn't right or wrong in itself. It is just what they are doing or saying. Look inside to see why a certain event seems to make you feel mad, or happy, or sad, then say, "What is true about me, about my *past,* is that I . . . ."

People say, "This pushes my (hot) buttons!" Why is that particular button hot? Of what does it reminded you? I found out a long time ago that the things about other people that push my buttons are almost always things I don't like about myself, or were once true of me when I was less skilled than I am now. They are my issues!

Pitfalls

1. *Don't give advice.* Here is a game to play in a group where a lot of advice is being given. Give everybody a 3x5 card. Tell them to write a person's name on the top and then write the advice they want to give to that person. Let them fill one side of the card. When everybody has finished, ask them to now read the card out loud, substituting their own name for the one they wrote at the top of the card. Most people will be amazed that the advice fits them so well. Try it.

Advice for others felt strongly is often advice for yourself, or what you might do, but that is not very good advice for another person. Advice giving puts you one-up, signals a power game, establishes your superior rank, and is counter to a truthful open relationship. Only give advice if asked, or with permission.

2. *Don't be a caretaker.* Whereas caring is a good thing, caretaking isn't unless it is actively sought. Caretaking is often a way of avoiding your own emotions and your own truth.

3. *Thinking you understand when you don't.* Sometimes we listen and nod our heads like we understand it all, but often we are making assumptions that the other's experience is just like ours. It rarely is. Check it out, ask questions. Mirror back what you have heard and ask if you understand. As Steven Covey writes, "understand first, and then seek to be understood".

4. *Judgment, making everything right or wrong.* Actually it seems so clear to us at times that the other person is right or wrong, but guess what? It is just an assumption. It is true that our sensory systems give qualitative experiences and our brains are wired to avoid pain and discomfort, things taste and smell bad. Maybe there are generally more pleasing sounds and sights.

Applied to relationships, these easily lead to judgments.   But judgments are most often generalizations from a few instances in certain circumstances.   People are not always only as we perceive them, especially those we know in only one context, like work. People act differently in different settings, work, family, leisure, with peers, with parents, with people of status.   The demands are different, and the taboos are different.

It's okay to be discerning, to note differences, to experience feelings in the face of others ways, but judgment puts people in a box and doesn't let them have a way to get out.   *Suspend judgment.*

Temporarily put those prejudices and old memories aside so you can listen and hear. Reflect back what you heard, to see if you got it right.

In the formulated process for assertion, you describe the behavior you observe, and then share how you feel when that happens. The key to this feeling statement is how vulnerable the confronter/asserter makes her/himself. Why is it important to demonstrate vulnerability when you are asking other people to change? The answer is that if they detect blame or judgment they will respond negatively to you and never change (The Fundamental Relationship Error, Ross, 2009). Normally these assertions and confrontations are aggressive and escalate differences. Blame and judgment are commonplace. In the world of dialogic truth, there is no room for blame or judgment.

Conclusion

Dialogic truth means that we say our truth in such a way as to continue the dialogue. We say our truth as a gift to the other person, and we give it in the spirit of opening the relationship for growth. At work, we establish community, trust, and respect for the talents and creative abilities of our co-workers. At home, and in our personal relationships, we overcome the separation and fragmentation that comes with guarded communications, lies, or manipulation. At the crux of it the truth does make us free.

References: A Casual Bibliography

David Bohm, *Wholeness and the Implicate Order*, New York: Arc Paperbacks, 1983.

David Bohm, *Unfolding Meaning: A Weekend of Dialogue with David Bohm*, New York: Arc Paperbacks, 1987.

David Bohm and J. Krishnamurti, *The Ending of Time*, San Francisco: Harper and Row, 1985.

David Bohm and F. David Peat, *Science, Order and Creativity*, New York: Bantam, 1987.

David Bohm and Mark Edwards, *Changing Consciousness*, San Francisco: Harper: San Francisco, 1991.

David Bohm, *On Dialogue.* [from David Bohm Seminars, P.O. Box 1452, Ojai, CA 93023.]

Peter Block, *Stewardship: Choosing Service over Self-interest*, San Francisco: Berrett-Koehler, 1993.

Patrick de Mare, *Koinonia: From Hate, through Dialogue to Culture in the Large Group,* New York: Karnac Books, 1991.

William Isaac, "Dialogue: The Power of Collective Thinking", *The System Thinker,* V.4, No.3, Cambridge: Pegasus Communications, 1993.

Ellinor, Linda, and Gerard, Glenna, *Dialogue: Rediscover the Transforming Power of Conversation*, Wiley, 1998.

Arnold Mindell, *Sitting In The Fire*, Lao Tse Press, Oregon, 1995.

Charles M. Savage, *Fifth Generation Management*, Maynard, MA: Digital Press, 1990.

Peter Senge, *The Fifth Discipline,* New York: Doubleday, 1990.

=====

1. David Bohm Seminars in Ojai distributes audio tapes, video tapes, transcripts of seminars and conversations, and several book length monographs by David Bohm.

2. "The System Thinker,' is a monthly newsletter published by Pegasus Communications, Cambridge, MA.

Suggested Readings.

Books:

Bohm, David and Edwards, Mark, *Changing Consciousness, Exploring the Hidden Source of the Social, Political and Environmental Crises Facing our World*, Pegasus, New York, NY. 1992.

Bohm, David, *On Dialogue,* David Bohm Seminars. Ojai, CA.

Bohm, David, *Unfolding Meaning: A weekend of Dialogue with David Bohm*, Ark Paperbacks, 1985.

Ellinor, Linda and Gerard, Glenna, *Dialogue: Rediscover the Transforming Power of Conversation*, Wiley, 1998.

Freidman, Maurice, *Dialogue and the Human Image Beyond Humanistic Psychology*. Sage Publications, Newbury Park, CA 1992.

Huang-Nissen, Sally, *Dialogue Groups: A Practical Guide to Facilitate Diversity Conversations,* Medicine Bear Publishing, 1999.

Jaworski, Joseph, *Synchronicity*, Berrett-Koehler, San Francisco, CA 1996.

Johnston, Charles M., M.D. *Necessary Wisdom, Meeting the Challenge of a New Cultural Maturity,* ICD Press. Seattle, WA. 1991.

Ross, Doug, *Make It Last: Loving Relationships,* Createspace.com, 2009.

Senge, Peter M. *The Fifth Discipline: The Art and Practice of the Learning Organization,* Doubleday/Currency, New York. 1990.

Wheatley, Margaret J. *Leadership and the New Science,* Berrett-Koehler, 1992.

Articles:

Vision/Action: The Journal of the Bay Area OD Network. Volume 13, No.2. Summer of 1994. This entire issue is devoted to dialogue, with articles by Doug Ross, Glenna Gerard and Linda Teurfs from the Center for Dialogic Communication, as well as many others.

Chawla, Sarita. *Dialogue: The Language of Community.* Vision/Action. Volume 13, No.4. Winter, 1994.

Gerard, G. *A Practice Field for Creating Community at Work*. At Work: Stories of Tomorrow's Workplace, March/April, 1993.

Isaacs, William N. *Taking Flight: Dialogue, Collective Thinking, and Organizational Learning.* Organizational Dynamics, 1993.

Schein, Edgard H. *On Dialogue, Culture, and Organizational Learning*. Organizational Dynamics, 1993.

Teurfs, Linda. *Finding a Shared Meaning: Reflections on Dialogue*. An interview with Linda Teurfs, by Jean Wielder; *Seeds of Unfolding: Spiritual Ideas for Daily Living*, Volume II, No. 1, 1994

Teurfs, Linda. *Moving from Blame to Dialogue,* Perspective, Association for Humanistic Psychology, July 1992.

A Sweat

I give up control
Release the need for my way
To be your way.

-DAR

About the Contributors

Michael Baroff - Now an independent consultant working with children, Michael was president of The Association for Humanistic Psychology, and is a member of the Council for the Center for Dialogic Communication. He resides and works in the Los Angeles Area.

David Bohm - (deceased) Bohm is the godfather of dialogue. He applies quantum physics to understanding how groups unfold meaning. He was deeply committed to peace in the world.

Linda Ellinor - Founding partner of The Dialogue Group, Linda is a trainer working with The Center for Creative Leadership. Linda is on the Board of the Center for Dialogic Communication. She resides with her dear son Colin in Orange County, CA.

Glenna Gerard - Founding Partner of The Dialogue Group, Glenna trains and consults for Interaction Associates in San Francisco, and is on the Board of the Center for Dialogic Communication. She resides in Ojo Caliente, MN, on sacred land.

Markus Hauser - Marcus lives and works in Vienna, Austria. He is an organizational consultant in private practice.

Anna May Simms - Anna May is a teacher and spiritual guide. She has brought dialogue to children in LA area schools, and is a member of the Center for Dialogic Communication Board.

Doug Ross is a University Professor of Psychology, an Organizational Development business consultant (Collaborative Solutions, Sarasota, FL) and a writer. His email is doug@doug-ross.com, and his web address is www.doug-ross.com .

3582667